M000279179

PARDON ME

the memoir of a reasonable man

James Gordon

James Gordon

ISBN: 9781667811994
eBook ISBN: 978166782007

As told to Dana Goolsby

Editor's Note: The names, details, and circumstances may have been altered to protect the privacy of those mentioned in this publication.

See my Facebook page:
Pardon Me: The memoir of a reasonable man by James Gordon for pictures associated with time periods in this book.

Cover Photo taken by James Gordon (1972) using a three-way mirror while in Germany—his first selfie.

This book is dedicated to my children

&

Governor Edwin Edwards.

Table of Contents

INTRODUCTION 1

Chapter One: Cut Off 9

Chapter Two: The Ties That Bind 19

Chapter Three: Prepare for Take Off 33

Chapter Four: Off to The Races 43

Chapter Five Losing My Religion 61

Chapter Six: Hash on Hand 73

Chapter Seven: The High Life 85

Chapter Eight: A Big Deal 101

Chapter Nine: Odyssey... 111

Chapter Ten: The Whole Twenty........................... 127

Chapter Eleven: I Beg My Pardon......................... 143

Chapter Twelve: Pardon My Pardon 157

Chapter Thirteen: Chasing My Tail to Find Me 167

Chapter Fourteen: You Never Know....................... 175

INTRODUCTION

"You should write a book," friends said. So, I did, and now they ask why I waited so long. I am a natural born storyteller who happened to live a very interesting life which has given me a multitude of stories to tell. Some sound a lot like tall tales, and if I spun them at all you wouldn't know it because the truth is standalone outlandish. My story is tragic, victorious, and true. It was rare to share my life story with someone who didn't immediately suggest that I should write a book.

When I began putting the book together, my editor asked me, "Why are you writing this book?" That was a first. In that moment I realized I did not know exactly why, other than for the fact that people said I should.

For the next year, I pondered that question, and eventually settled on the seemingly simple purpose of sharing. But sharing isn't simple in any sense of the word. Above all reasons, simple and complex, this book is ultimately for my children. I am seventy-two years old, and I've never shared my life story with them. It occurred to me that my children needed the opportunity to know more about my life, so that they might better understand their own. In spite of all the obstacles, particularly me, all three of my children are brilliant and successful adults, and I cherish each of them. I am also eternally grateful that they have allowed me to be part of their lives. I am fully aware that my mistakes and the consequences I faced impacted their lives, and that it was hard. I will always wish I could change this part of the past more than the rest. Beyond that, it is my hope that my life story might inspire, or at the very least, entertain someone. It is not lost on me that I am not the only person who has experienced self-induced hardship, nor am I the only person who has ever had to pay a steep price for the choices they made. However, I do believe I am in a small group of people who paid the price and recaptured my life. "Paying the price" for mistakes is a tough gig, but the real work lies in how we navigate the situation. Most people never come out on the other side of a setback of such magnitude, and even more never obtain any level of success once they've settled their debt. The fact that I did overcome is viewed as a miracle by many people. What the heck is a miracle anyway? Do miracles come out of thin air? Does a deity in the sky hand them out? And if so, how does one qualify to receive one? Why do some people get miracles and others do not? Do you remember the saying, "There's no such thing as a free lunch?" There is no such thing as a free lunch. Perhaps free to you, but not free. Somewhere along the line someone paid for something. The same applies to miracles. Someone somewhere worked to make a "miracle" happen. So, when someone says, "It's a miracle," that translates to – "Over time many people have contributed to the manifestation of this accomplishment through hard work." You might be thinking, "Damn, James, that's a real downer." If your bubble has been burst, allow me to pick you up and dust you off with the secret to achieving anything, even "miracles." No matter who you are, where you are in your life, or how far and hard you've fallen, absolutely anything you want is possible and obtainable if you follow three easy steps. The steps will seem so simple, that most people won't believe it, let alone buy into it.

2

This book is not a cookbook filled with recipes for success or self-help, but I do believe in and live by the three key ingredients, which you will read about in Chapter One, that are necessary to manifest miracles and transform lives. Anything is possible, but no one is going to show up at your front door and hand you your goals and dreams on a silver platter with no effort on your part. Retirement is the next threshold I will cross and one of the final freedoms I will experience, which has ultimately allowed me to tell my story. Despite everything I've overcome, the lives I've saved, and the fences I've mended, my professional life just didn't leave room for me to tell my story authentically. The book has been in the making for several years but is wrapping up just as my career is winding down. Retirement won't just be the freedom to do with my days as I please, it will be the freedom to share without repercussions and suffering. I do not regret waiting to tell my story until I've retired because I have loved my career. I was called into this line of work, and I worked hard to get where I am. I chose to wait it out because I know how hard it is for people to forgive and accept. That's the nature of the beast because in general people feel better when someone is beneath them in some way. It can be impossible to redeem yourself with some people, and I decided I was done explaining myself and my story to people who cannot see past mistakes, even when change is obvious, and years have passed.

I owe much to many people, but I want to specifically thank my children Tracy and Brian for giving me a second chance. I know that what happened to me also happened to them, and that their experience was much different than my own but just as hard. I want to thank my first wife, Linda, for taking care of our children. I regret the hardship I caused in her life and despite any effort to make it up to her, I know I can't. I also want to thank my second wife, Melanie, whom I am no longer married to, but we remain best friends and I know we always will. We've been through a lot, and she suffered right along with everyone else because of my mistakes. I would also like to thank John Hydell, who gave me the opportunity to get back into medicine. He was instrumental in my success and in a lot of ways I owe my success to him for giving me that one chance to redeem myself. I would also like to thank Dr. David Johnson, who hired me as a nurse practitioner in Tyler, Texas when the State of Louisiana would not license me. I am also grateful to have worked with Dr. Jonathan Markowitz, one of the most brilliant doctors I have ever met. Not only was he my friend, but also an important mentor. I am confident today in my profession because of him. I truly feel honored to have worked so many years with so many great people, from nurses to doctors. And lastly, I would like to thank Brenda Boyd for pushing me to write this book and introducing me to my editor, Dana Goolsby.

PARDON

ME

the memoir of a reasonable man

James Gordon

Chapter One: Cut Off

Aging, achieved gracefully or otherwise, is a gift. The ups, the downs, the adventures and misadventures, the people who come in and out of your life, the heartache and physical pain—sometimes one and the same—are the ingredients of the gift. It's actually quite similar to a miracle. A miracle is the actual happening, and everything before the miracle is the hard work, dedication, and sometimes pure luck that ultimately comes together at the right time to produce a miracle, be that as it may, as it's different for everyone. By the time you reach a certain age, you should be able to reflect on your time and analyze the total sum of your life to formulate the person you became. It's a miracle in every sense of the word that I've come to be a man of seventy years and counting. Seven decades of life experiences, packed full of highs and lows, have created the person I am today. And yet, I am still learning and growing, and therefore, the man I am today will not be the man I am in the future. Everyone changes over time, or at least we should hope to, and hopefully for the better. When my mind is drawn back to the man I used to be, I am reminded of many people, places, and things that are no longer in my life, but I also distinctly recall where I came from, what I went through, and how I got where I am today. And today I am living my best and most authentic life.

I believe that anyone can do anything. It is that simple. Every goal is attainable if you do three things. You have to want it; you have to believe you're going to accomplish it; and you have to wake up every day and do the things necessary to obtain it. People often shortchange themselves by lowering their goals and expectations. It's harder to fail when the bar is lowered, but there is nothing wrong with failure. The most important thing is just showing up.

In order to understand a person's life, your own or someone else's, you have to look at the big picture. A snapshot may say a thousand words, but it doesn't tell you the whole story. Everyone has a story and some of us have many, and over the years those stories change as we change. Some stories grow more colorful after several retellings, while other stories are watered down for secrecy and self-preservation. For many years people have encouraged me to write a book. My real-life stories have inspired, entertained, and intrigued many people over the years, but the sole purpose of sharing my life story is so that my children may know me better, understand more and perhaps better, about the life events that unfolded and molded us all into the people we are today.

My story began on Bayou Lafourche, Louisiana in 1949, near a menagerie of little communities, in a little town called Golden Meadow. Golden Meadow was just down the road from Cut Off, where generations of my family had settled years and years prior to my arrival. Just about thirty-three miles south of New Orleans as the crow flies, Cut Off was named for a cutoff canal that was intended to connect Bayou Lafourche to New Orleans via Lake Salvador. And it was only about 45 miles away from the end of the world, also known as Grand Isle. Looking back, at that time the area seemed relatively untouched compared what it is like today, although it is still a small town. It was a natural paradise, perfect for fishing, hunting, trapping, boating, swimming, and just about any other thing a young boy or outdoorsman could want to do.

It was a different time. People were poor. The Depression was still fresh on people's minds and communities were still recovering. World War II had ended, and people only had their families and communities. It was at a time when Americans were not inundated with news and media. Most people didn't even have a television, and the ones who did only got three channels if they were lucky. Cut Off was still really, well, cut off from the world at that time, and life passed a little slower. Cut Off and neighboring communities like LaRose, Thibodaux, and Golden Meadow were a melting pot of tradition, heritage, and bayou culture. These tight knit communities were still new in relation to the area's history. Generations of families have called this quaint, natural area home for many years, and my family was one of them, but the schoolhouse was only twenty years old. It was a time when nature still had the upper hand and populations were still low. No one locked their doors. Hell, we didn't even have a lock on our door. When we left town, we left our doors open. If someone needed something while we were away, perhaps a cup of sugar, they went in and got it and paid you back later. People sent their kids outside to play all day, which sometimes lasted well into the night with kids riding their bikes up and down the street, playing hide and go seek, and looking for new things to discover. We were all about being outside, and we were out there constantly. From the moment you woke up in the morning, your mom would throw you out of the house. She'd call you back in for lunch, then throw you out again or make you take a nap if you didn't want to go. They didn't care what you did, as long as you did it outside. There was no option to sit around inside the house and watch television, nor would it have ever been permitted. It was all about playing and we played hard. We wore the tires off bicycles and never came in before they made us. No one panicked when they had not seen their kids all day. But that was a different time.

Everything still seemed mostly undisturbed in the bayou. It hadn't been that long since Highway 1 had come into existence, connecting Shreveport to New Orleans, and paving the way for rural communities, quite literally, to reach hospitals, schools and voting booths. In 1928, Louisiana elected one of the most charismatic and controversial politicians in Louisiana's history. Governor Huey Long ordered the construction of thousands of miles of roads, numerous bridges, and multiple municipal buildings. Travelers could get from Shreveport to New Orleans in a day; a trip that had previously taken farmers several days to connect their crops and goods to market, and a trip that always ran the risk of a rain delay. Most of the state's roads linking major towns were little more than rutted winding dirt roads that turned into thick, unforgiving mud when it rained. It wasn't uncommon for travelers to be stuck for days until the roads dried enough to continue. The Governor's ambitious road building program doubled the state's highway system in four years and contributed to Louisiana's strength through the Great Depression. Long, whose campaign slogan was "Every man a king!" became known as the "poor man's champion," and he gave himself the nickname "Kingfish." There are many varied tales about Long, but my favorite is based on a fictional tale with a character loosely based on the Governor in "All the King's Men," by Robert Penn Warren. The movie tells a tale about how Long got his ambitious highway system completed in record time. The story goes, the governor wanted his B line highway from Grand Isle to Shreveport, but the powers that be in state government didn't want to pony up the cash to complete the road in Long's record setting time frame. Long ordered a mile of asphalt, followed by a mile of gravel, from Grand Isle to Shreveport. Imagine what a pain in the ass, literally, it would have been to be cruising along in your 1932 Model B Ford, going from pavement to gravel over and over every mile of the way. Legend has it, that was enough to piss off the good people of Louisiana who in turn complained so much they went ahead and funded the entire road project.

I feel very lucky to have grown up in rural southeast Louisiana. My memories of the area's natural beauty are grandiose, and when I replay them in my mind, they feel like scenes from an old familiar movie. I can recall with such ease the details of those days of innocence. On a rainy day we would run down to the shipyard and get the guys at the shop to saw off the ends of old wooden blocks. And just like that, we had our own seaworthy vessels to pull down the waterfilled ditches along the side of the road. The kind of freedom we experienced in those days is something we couldn't even give our children just one generation later, and certainly something the youth of today or the future will never know. We spent hours and hours outside and did not have a single care in the world, and no one worried about us. We made clubhouses out of everything. We upcycled, reclaimed, repurposed, anything we could get our hands on. We made treehouses 30 to 40 feet in the air, we transformed an old cistern that was turned sideways into a clubhouse, complete with bunk beds. Once we even turned a chicken coop into a clubhouse, but I ended with histo spots in my eyes from that project. Despite the histo spots, it was a great time to be a kid in a great environment.

I think back to that freedom and see myself as a boy of about 12 years old in a small, handmade boat called a pirogue, that my uncle made for my older cousin, Ronnie. He never used it so I asked my aunt if I could, and she obliged. On the back of the pirogue there was a small 5.5 horsepower Briggs and Stratton motor connected to a straight drive shaft, with a wooden stick on the rudder. I would wind the string around the pully, then give it a good yank, and quickly grab the handle because it took off immediately. My cousin Morris also had a pirogue. His was bigger with a 9.5 horsepower Briggs and Stratton motor. We would shove off at 6:00 a.m. in our shorts with our fishing lines in tow. We would travel all over the marshland, winding in and out of the cypress trees and gliding through the murky waters that extended along the Bayou Lafourche. We navigated those little pirogues among tugboats and shrimp boats on the river and canals, and we fished from old oil derricks and abandoned barges in the swamps during the warm months. When it was cold, we made our way through the swamps to hunt for ducks and to trap muskrats and nutria. It was beautiful back in those swamps, and we never missed an opportunity for adventure. At the tender ages of 11 and 12 we were our own captains and the masters of our own fate.

Cajun traditions and heritage influenced every aspect of our lives on the bayou, holidays notwithstanding, and perhaps even celebrated with a little more coon ass flare. One of my favorite traditions fell during the early summer. We would take one or two boats across the bayou to Golden Meadow. There was a bakery there called Dufrene's Bakery that we bought fresh hot bread from just as it was coming out of the oven. From there, we took our bread and boats through the canal to the last bridge over Bayou La Fourche, which we always called "pointe de la saucisse," which translates to "point of the sausage." As we entered "Tee Lack" (Little Lake), we would drop the trawl as we crossed to Bayou Cafe`, where my uncle's hunting camp was located. When we arrived at the camp, the trawl was dumped into a sorting box. My mom and her sisters would sort through the troll, discarding trash fish and debris. While they made a rich, thick tomato sauce, they would peel the shrimp and get everything ready to cook a huge batch of seafood spaghetti. Everything from shrimp to crab halves, to oysters we brought from home, and just about anything else we caught was combined and served over a bed of spaghetti along with hot French bread. By around 8 p.m. everyone was well on their way to being full. Those were great times.

During those days of uninhibited natural freedom, I also enjoyed time with my grandparents, and great-grandparents. Two of the best and most vivid memories I have from my great grandparents are their solid dirt yard and their mandarin orange trees. Every spring the orange trees would flower, and the scent filled the air, and by summertime we were peeling and eating oranges off the trees.

My grandparents' and great-grandparents' lives were a distinct reflection of three eras— Pre-Depression, Depression, and WWII. My great-grandmother had long silver hair twisted into a bun. She often wore an old bonnet to work in the yard and regularly sat on the back steps of the house smoking out of a corn cob pipe. She only spoke about ten words in English, and my great-grandfather never spoke in English. My grandfather spoke English out of necessity. He worked with people who spoke only in English and had to learn quickly. You have to admire people who speak more than one language. It's an incredible form of adaptation and speaks to what humans can do when they are able to communicate. We spoke French when we talked to our grandparents back then, but with the passage of time and their passing, we slowly and sadly let the language go.

What is now part of the strategic oil reserve for the nation was once my grandfather's family land, from which he made his living trapping and fishing. My grandfather was one of twelve children, and due to the size of the family there ended up being about 150 heirs involved in the marshland, however, eminent domain eventually took most of the land. My mother received a very small check for her portion, which she never cashed.

That said, time changes and waits for no one.

We had a lot of fun with my grandparents, and I am thankful to have the experiences I did with them as a child. The life I experienced with them was nearing extinction, or may have even been extinct already, but because we were poor, we still lived a very old-fashioned lifestyle. At any rate, certain practices and ways of living died with my grandparents in that bayou. Despite my parents having been immersed in old cultural ways of life, and even though my generation was exposed directly to it, those old ways live only in my mind's eye now.

I can almost see and smell my grandfather's pig pen. Every spring he bought a young hog that everyone in our neighborhood family fed and ate. My grandfather would put a slop bucket at everyone's house, and all our scraps went into the bucket at the end of the day. He would collect the slop buckets and fatten up the spring pig until the fall. When autumn arrived, they picked a Saturday for the slaughter and fed the hog corn for three weeks prior. When slaughter Saturday finally rolled around, we would wake up early and go push the hog through the gate, where someone would then shoot him with a .22 rifle, and then slide him down the ramp to bleed out for blood stew in my grandmother's octagon shaped pot. Everything got used; nothing was wasted. We used wood scraps from the shipyard to boil the water needed to shave the hog with a cane knife. We used the feet, brain, ears, and intestines. The adults always gave the hog's bladder to us kids to play with, which might sound odd, unless you know that you can use a straw to blow it up and transform it into a kickball! We made everything from boudin to hog head cheese with that spring hog and had a good time doing it. I remember watching the outer lining melt down for cracklin's, which were scooped out into a cheesecloth to drain the oil that we used to fry all our food for the rest of the year. My grandparents were resourceful and never wasted anything. They made the absolute best of what they had, and that included the time they spent with us. Our family time was rich in ways I cannot recreate.

Growing up within eyeshot of most of my family also enriched my childhood in a way that is mostly, if not completely, obsolete today. Most of my family lived within spitting distance from one another. The way our neighborhood was situated, my mother's parents lived closest to Highway 308 in a Creole shotgun house, and their three children purchased lots behind them. My oldest aunt, whose husband was a ship builder, lived behind my grandparents and operated a shipyard next door. Our house was next, and then finally my mom's youngest sister lived at the end with her family. My mom and each of her sisters had two to four children, so I grew up close with my cousins. Everyone was close figuratively and literally! We saw our extended family every day—intentionally. My grandmother and her three daughters got together every day at 2:00 p.m. for coffee in the afternoon. They called it "petite goût," which means "a little taste." They would sip coffee and talk about their day or how much clothes they had washed. While they sipped coffee, we played outside. We were one big neighborhood of relatives.

Chapter Two: The Ties That Bind

As much as we were one big family on the block, I always felt like my family just didn't quite fit in. We were the black sheep of our devout Cajun Catholic family. My mother's first marriage had soured, resulting in abuse, and ending in divorce after she had her first child, Kathleen, who we called Katie. After my mother divorced her abuser, she was no longer permitted to take communion with the Catholic church. Divorce was the ultimate taboo at that time, and looked down upon, and therefore, so were we.

My mother was a wonderful woman; if she had flaws, I couldn't see them. Even to this day, her memory conjures up the spirit of unconditional love and happiness. Everyone thinks their mother hung the moon, but my mom really did. She was a lovely woman with a heart of gold.

One of three sisters, the Gisclair girls were tightknit, but my mother's first marriage would forever change the family dynamics. She had an 8th grade education, which she acquired from the folks who ran the local store and the local school. That was the highest level of education available to her. What she lacked in education she made up for in charm and looks, as evidenced by the sheer number of suitors who crossed the bayou in pirogues to court her. By the time she was about sixteen, a fellow by the name of St. Pierre had snatched her up and married her. They were married in the Catholic church, in a traditional Catholic wedding ceremony. The honeymoon phase seemed to have ended no sooner than it began, perhaps just long enough for them to conceive my sister Katie. Maybe it didn't, but it is easier for me to believe she was conceived in love, or at least something like it.

My father, George Wesley Gordon, was from Clara, Mississippi. He was from a broken home; his parents owned a hardware store but lost everything during the Great Depression. After his parents' sudden passing, he and his older brother and sister became orphans. Not too much time ticked by before trouble found my father. His older brother was a moonshiner and had him run shine between Clara and Gulfport. By the age of 13 he was arrested for transporting moonshine and sent to reform school. I remember him talking about having to fight the biggest guy there on the first day. He stayed there until he was 17. At that time, he joined the Navy and became a medical corpsman. He was sent to Panama City, Florida, where he served in WWII. After his service in the Navy, he found work as an offshore roughneck working in the Gulf of Mexico, off the coast of Louisiana where he eventually met my mother. He happened into the store where my mother worked, and they hit it off. A lot of men came calling on my mother, so much that the store owner made it her business to help keep the suitors in line or run them off altogether. My mother would reveal to her which suitor she might have some interest in, as well as those of which she had absolutely no interest. If an unwanted suitor showed up to flirt with my mother, the owner would tell him point blank not to bother her because she did not like him. When my father came calling, my mother and the store owner allowed him to flirt with her.

He eventually gave them his name and raised Katie as his own, and he allowed her to continue being raised in the Catholic Church. The only problem was, the name he gave us was Gordon. My mother had been a Gisclair and everyone else had French names like Thibodeaux, Boudreaux, LeBlanc, Bourgeois, or Cormier. We were "the Gordons." It just didn't have the same ring to it. It somehow made me feel like less of a Coonass and more like an oddball. My parents got married and rented a little house. It wasn't long before their readymade family was extended by one. My arrival prompted my father to think about his old homestead in Clara, about 400 miles away. He travelled to Mississippi and tear down the old home place and bring it back to Cut Off to make it our home. Board by board he tore the old house down and drove the lumber back to Cut Off. There he constructed a very meager two-bedroom house with one bathroom. Over the years he added a kitchen, living room, and a hallway that led to two additional bedrooms. The house never changed again after that.

After my arrival in 1949, my sister Lillie was born two years later, then Patricia arrived just a few years after that. At the time Lillie was born my mother could not have imagined her fate was to become a caretaker for the rest of her life. No one knew exactly what was wrong with Lillie, but it seemed very similar to Downes Syndrome, and her IQ was about 65. It would be many, many years later before they discovered she had Williams Syndrome. Williams Syndrome is a genetic condition that is present at birth and even conception and is characterized by medical problems, including cardiovascular disease, developmental delays, and learning challenges. However, despite these extreme challenges, people with Williams Syndrome often have striking verbal abilities, highly social personalities, and oftentimes an affinity for music. One night, *20/20* featured someone who was a lot like Lillie—very personable and friendly but with a very low IQ—and mom knew the disease was the same thing Lillie had. Mom made sure she had a full and productive life. She dedicated her life to ensuring Lillie had a decent life. My parents put her in a school for children with special needs, and there Lillie thrived. She was taught to read and write, along with basic life skills. She joined the Bayou Bell Ringers, which was made up of all kinds of people with various special needs. They played for the U.S. President, and they traveled to places to perform. It was an incredible experience for her and our family.

Lillie, while innocent and sweet, was the source of a lot of added stress in my family. While my mom loved and cared for her, my dad often used her as a tool to insult the other children, but particularly me. For instance, if I struggled with something or couldn't catch on to something fast enough my father would say, "What are you, a retard? Your sister can even do that!" It was cruel on a lot of levels, but I never held it against Lillie. In fact, I have made sure Lillie has been and is well cared for after all these years. She has lived in a facility near me in Lindale until recently moving back to Cut Off to be closer to my sister, Patricia.

By the time I was about eight years old, my parents were dragging us to the Baptist church every time the doors were open. All they wanted to do or showed interest in from that point forward was church stuff. Church was a way of life and a connection to the world. Other connections and memberships my parents fostered included my father being a 32nd degree Mason and Shriner, and my mother belonged to the Eastern Stars. She was the oldest active member of the Eastern Stars in Louisiana when she died. People belonged to churches and clubs because it was the only social lifeline they had back then. There was nothing to do, so they joined social clubs with secret handshakes for socialization. It was all they had, and I am glad they had it.

My father was a hothead, drank too much, and was just generally an asshole. I like to think that my father loved us the best he could, but there was certainly room for improvement. I sometimes find myself defending and condemning him almost simultaneously. I tell myself he did the best he could, but I am never able to convince myself. He was rough around the edges at home, but well-liked in the community. He was a character, and he acquired a lot of nicknames. They called him "Greasy," "Greasy Gordon," and "Red." It was almost as if he was a different person with other people, and he reserved his hatefulness for his family. Much, much later in life I learned of his rumored affairs that took place before he "found the Lord." And because he had found the Lord, the rest of us had to also.

He was strict, and it seemed like every day he was home I got a beating with the belt. He was a hard man, and even harder on me than with the girls. Katie and Lillie never got spankings. Katie wasn't his biological child and therefore he did not discipline her the same, and Lillie didn't get in trouble for obvious reasons. Patricia and I were not so lucky. He chased me every day and when he caught me, he beat me for no particular reason, or sometimes for reasons that seemed less than justified. It was like clockwork. You always knew it was coming. Out of all four kids, Patricia, the youngest, had the hardest head of all. I always thought if he was going to kill one of us it would be her. One day, dad slapped Patricia's face, and in turn, she punched him square in his face. Being the baby of the family is probably the only thing that saved her. My mother was the only person who had any sort of control over my father, and the only person who was able to coax him into doing the right thing. In other words, she could stop him just before he killed you.

Katie and Lillie were exempt from my father's belt, but once when Katie was thirteen, she got a whipping from a priest at Catechism school. She could not remember all the information she was tasked with memorizing, and a priest decided she should be punished. Katie came home from school and had red marks all over her legs. My father asked her what the marks on her legs were from, and she explained that a priest had whipped her with a stick for failing to memorize all the information she had been assigned. He was enraged. He loaded up Katie, my mother, and the rest of us kids into the car and drove to the rectory. He knocked on the door and when the priest answered he escorted him out to the car where my mother and Katie were waiting. My father grabbed him by his smock and lifted him off the ground. His feet seemed to dangle from beneath his black robe of righteousness, as my father vowed to beat him to death if he ever laid another finger on Katie. I guess he figured if he couldn't whip her no one else ought to either.

Around age fourteen, Katie became a child bride to an older man who ran around on her and kept her at home. It didn't take long for her to have enough of it and divorce him, but reclaiming her life was not in the cards. Things never got easier.

My father worked in the oilfield offshore and then later as a nightshift gauger for an oil company called J.W. Meecham in Delta Farms, Louisiana. His shift was from 7 p.m. until 7 a.m., and on occasion we got to go to work with him. Sometimes one of my cousins would tag along and we would go night hunting. We rode in the back of the truck and stood on the toolbox. When dad pulled into the well sites with his lights blaring, the rabbits would freeze dead in their tracks, making them easy prey for us. I learned to drive there on Delta Farms. We had an old standard shift station wagon, and he let me drive it all over the place on those gravel roads while he was working.

He was a working man, and he was cheap. Innovative but cheap in ways, that looking back, I am surprised didn't get us killed. In his line of work there was an oil and gas separator that produced a byproduct called "drip gasoline," also known as "white gas." They collected it at work in 55-gallon drums. My dad would bring a drum home and run our vehicles off that white gas. It was so combustible that when you turned the ignition off, it had such a flash point that the engine kept running. When the 1957 Ford Station Wagon was running on white gas, you had to

25

put the car in gear and let the clutch out in order to bog down the engine enough to make it stop "dieseling," which is what an engine does when it runs without ignition. Dad had some relatives that lived about 400 miles away that he wanted to visit. He wasn't about to spend a dime at a gas station, so we loaded the 55-gallon drum of white gas into the back of the station wagon, propped it up on blocks and 2x4s, and away we went to our family reunion. When we got low on gas, we stopped and syphoned it from the drum that was sloshing around in the back. It's a wonder I can even recall this trip at all considering the overpowering fumes of white gas lingered the entire 400 miles. There we were cruising down the highway on white gas, just lucky we didn't go off like an atomic bomb. On the way home dad had to buy three dollars of gas. He was so pissed!

Dad was angry a lot and a rough man on a good day. He once went to New Orleans for Mardi Gras and got in a fist fight over beads. The cops came in to break it up and my father grabbed one of the officers by the shirt and tore it from his body, leaving them no choice but to billy club him down to the pavement. He received eight stitches, and he was ordered to pay a fine and purchase a new shirt for the officer he assaulted. They were used to people doing dumb shit in New Orleans, and that was exactly what this was—dumb shit that didn't amount to much, therefore they figured the punishment matched the crime well enough.

It was not unusual for my father to drop his family off somewhere while he got started on a binge. Once, he took my mom, sisters, and I, as well as my aunt and her kids to New

Orleans, where he left us at Audubon Park. While we enjoyed the park, he hit up the bars. As the day wore on, we had not seen any sign of him, and it was getting dark. The police were going to throw us out of the park by 8 p.m., but he showed up just in time to retrieve us. He was drunk as a skunk! My father did things his way, and if it wasn't his way, it was even harder.

My parents didn't seem to have a very loving or good relationship. It appeared that they "stayed together for the family." In reality, they probably stayed together due to lack of options. Mom was never particularly happy, but she had nowhere to go. She always just seemed to be waiting for it to end. They were pretty much polar opposites, and the way I felt about them was polar opposite.

By the time I was in high school, my mother had become a caretaker to more than Lillie. My father was around fifty years old when he was diagnosed with polycystic kidney disease and became disabled. Since he was a WWII veteran, his care and transportation were provided. He was transported to the VA Clinic in New Orleans three times a week for hemodialysis treatments. He needed knee surgery but was unable to have it due to his medical condition and his weak heart. While the VA picked up the tab and handled the medical my mother was tasked with every other element of caring for my father along with my handicapped sister at home.

A decade passed during which my mother was a caretaker for two very different people, with very different issues, when another issue arose. My sister Katie was diagnosed with sarcoidosis, an inflammatory disease that can affect multiple organs and tissues. She had the worst kind, pulmonary fibrosis, which is scarring of the lungs, often described as "leatherlike lungs." It completely crippled Katie. She spent about three months in an intensive care unit with a chest tube. They put in a Heimlich valve and sent her home with hospice. They had done all they could do for her. She died a horrible death, short of breath and constantly struggling for air until she finally passed away. I don't believe my mother ever really got over losing Katie that way. Any time anyone mentioned her name my mother always cried.

Five years after Katie passed, my father died. My mother never dated or remarried.

By this point, my mother had taken care of three immediate family members in bad health and buried two of them. I always recognized the goodness in my mother, probably because I saw how much she sacrificed for her family, and how she dedicated her own life to caring for others at the end of theirs, as well her commitment to Lillie. There really was not anything she would not do for you if she loved you. We were poor; we had what we needed and no more, but mom loved us enough to get through the hard times. My mother inspired me in so many ways, and as I've grown older, I can see that I followed her footsteps down the path of caring for others.

She was an intelligent woman despite not having much of a formal education and absolutely no one was better at a crossword puzzle. If you ever needed a six-letter word, she knew them all, and every definition! She eventually obtained her G.E.D., which she was extremely proud of. She didn't get behind the wheel of a car until she was almost 50 years old. Until I left for college, she had never seen a need to drive because there was always someone to do it for her and we lived within walking distance from everything we needed. But with her able children growing up and leaving home, she decided to take a class and learn how to drive. Two years after she became a licensed driver, I got in the car with her to take a drive. She was speeding and driving wildly. I finally had to tell her to pull over. Reluctant and a little pissed, she asked why I wanted her to pull over. I said, "Because you're driving like a fucking maniac!" She did not pull over and said she could handle it. Suddenly our roles were reversed, and I found myself scolding her and reminding her that she needed to be careful because she had only been driving two years.

My mother went on to live to be eighty-nine years old. She ended up with rapid onset dementia and it was so severe she could not manage it. I would go home to visit her, and I could tell things were changing. She was aware that there was less life ahead of her and more behind her. She would often tell me that she knew she was going to die soon, and she would often follow that statement with, "I just don't want to go cuckoo." Looking back, I think she knew that she was presenting signs of dementia, but once it started the rest happened swiftly. She didn't want to go to a nursing home; no one really does. My sister Patricia tried to keep her from going into a nursing home, but it proved to be too difficult. Mother had become violent, and even violent to Lillie, who she had loved and cared for unconditionally. I always wondered if there were repressed feelings of resentment towards Lillie peeking through the confusion and rage. Her lifelong independent nature reared its head when the battle for the car keys finally ensued. She refused to give them up. When she was straight, she thought she was straight all the time, and she couldn't recognize the difficulties she was having even though she didn't seem to know anyone anymore. Everyone had become a stranger.

About two months after my last trip to see her, Patricia called and said we needed to make adjustments to mom's medication. By this time, my sister could not leave my mother at all, and if she did, she had to ask the neighbor to look in on her while she was away. Patricia went on to tell me that if mom slept, she slept 13 to 14 hours at a time, and recently she had taken a serious fall. Bloody and confused after falling from the backsteps, she wandered over to a neighbor's house where she told them a Jehovah's Witness came to her door and assaulted her. There was blood everywhere at the house and on her, and still she resisted going to the hospital.

I told Patricia to bring her to Tyler, Texas where I lived and worked. When they arrived, my mother was a completely different person than the woman I had known all my life and seen just two months earlier. She could recall some things from my childhood, but she remembered Patricia and I as a couple rather than as siblings. She was too far gone, and I was terribly embarrassed. I apologized to my mother and sister for letting it get so bad, even though there was nothing I could have done about it. I arranged for her to see a friend of mine who was a neurologist, then I made the decision to place her in a nursing home in Metairie, a suburb of New Orleans. She moved in on a Sunday and the following Tuesday I drove down to see her. She was in a wheelchair tied to another wheelchair, with a board strapped across her to keep her from falling out of the chair. She looked at me, never once recognizing me, while she picked and pulled at the restraint. She died the next morning at 4 a.m. We did have the opportunity to tell her goodbye, but she had already been gone a long time. She had no idea what was happening or who we were. It was a relief when she did go. I would have smothered her with a pillow if I could have to stop the disease from ravishing her the way it did. Watching her mind disappear was torture. It was a bittersweet ending.

My parents were strikingly different people. It appears that opposites do attract, but relationships built on opposites are not usually timeless love stories for the ages, and oftentimes the turmoil left in their wake falls mostly to the children to reckon with for decades to come. Considering my own life choices, my spouses and lovers, and my children, I am left to believe that this cannot be helped based on one thing—"humanness." We are all just human, although sometimes it seems like some of us are more human than others. We all eventually recognize our parents, and sometimes our grandparents, within ourselves. With any luck, we recognize the things about our parents that we do not want to carry forward into our future lives, with our future selves and families. And if we aren't lucky, we make the same mistakes our parents made and the path we carve out isn't our own path at all, but rather it's just an extension of the road paved long before our feet even hit the path.

31

That said, I attempted to stray from every path, every trail, and every road my family had forged. I jumped the track, took shortcuts, and went off the rail. I intended to do it my way, and I did. Looking back now I can see that I made a lot of the same mistakes that my parents made. I ended up a lot more like both of my parents than I had ever imagined possible. Only when we reflect are we able to figure that out.

Chapter Three: Prepare for Take Off

As soon as I started school I struggled. Luckily, by the time I started first grade, they finally realized I couldn't see the chalk board and moved me to the front of the classroom. My parents eventually made an appointment for me with an eye doctor. The closest eye doctor was seventy miles away in New Orleans, and you couldn't get the glasses the same day. You had to wait three weeks and come back to get fitted and pick them up. Getting glasses was a game changer. I started doing better in school and figured out I could make money at recess by lighting small grass fires in the schoolyard with my glasses. I was far sighted, and my glasses were super thick. They were exactly what you think of when you hear the phrase "coke bottle glasses." Once, I had a pair of tortoise shell glasses that got run over during a game of cops and robbers. When I told my parents what had happened, my dad and I spent the entire weekend going through every single blade of grass in that ditch. We hunted and picked up every single tiny piece, with the exception of one small piece missing along the top that was about an eighth of an inch. We glued all the pieces back together and I put tape over the piece that was missing. You didn't just run out and get a new pair of glasses back then. It was a big deal to have to go to all the way to New Orleans for a new pair of glasses, and we didn't exactly have the extra money.

I talked way too much, but my grades were good. I had Attention Deficit/Hyperactivity Disorder (ADHD), but back then no one knew what that was. In those days, teachers just thought you were an asshole kid who wouldn't shut up and needed to be punished. In the fifth grade I had a strict male teacher. He was balding with a crewcut hairdo, a real clean cut, hardnosed, straight-shooting guy. He got so sick of me talking in class that he assigned me to copy the entire Webster's Dictionary by hand on paper. The task seemed impossible, so I never even started. Every day the teacher would ask me how much I had done, and every day I would say, "Nothing! I haven't even started." He finally called my father and told on me. My father asked me why I was not doing my punishment work, to which I explained that it was impossible for a human to hand copy the Webster's Dictionary, and since I would never be able to finish, I asked why I should even start. It seemed logical at the time. I never ended up doing the assignment because it was an impossible assignment, and they knew it. The teacher assigned some other sort of punishment work, and it must have met my standards, although I cannot recall. All I know is that I didn't handwrite Webster's Dictionary.

All the little surrounding towns seemed to merge seamlessly together. The minute you left one little town you were immediately in the next little town. For a long time, each little town had its own school district. I went to Galliano Middle School for grades seven through nine. That was about the time I conjured up one of my favorite and perhaps oldest jokes. To this day, people ask me where I am from, I almost always tell them, "I'm from Circumcised, Louisiana, but we just call it Cut Off for short." It makes complete sense that I developed this joke in junior high, and if you know me, it makes complete sense that I still tell it all these years later.

Middle school was a relatively insignificant era in my life, at least within the realm of higher learning, but within my neighborhood there was always something to learn. I was shy and reserved but always had friends. When I turned twelve, I took a weekend job at a local gas station washing and vacuuming cars and pumping gas. I earned one dollar per hour. I wasn't afraid of work, and I loved being able to make my own money. I worked all through high school at gas stations. Of course, my main job was to get out of high school and get out of Cut Off.

My Uncle Dudley had an old standard shift Chevrolet that he bought in 1952. He kept that car even after he bought a new Dodge, complete with wings and all that jazz. Just as middle school was wrapping up, I got my driver's license. One day my aunt asked me to go pick up the kids from Galliano Middle School, and I was all too happy to do it. There I was, fifteen years old, driving the hell out of that 52' Chevy. I was peeling out on every street, spinning wheels, and burning rubber. I was tearing up the roads acting a fifteen-year-old fool, because I was. When I got to the middle school, it was time to really show off. I revved up the engine so much that when I let go of the clutch the tires started squealing. As I peeled out, I heard something "POP!" I had broken the drive shaft. I was going to have to make a call. Back then you couldn't just call someone on your cell phone to come help you. I had to go into the office and use the phone. And just getting to the phone didn't mean someone

35

would pick up on the other end. Whoever you were calling might be outside or not even at home. Sometimes getting in touch with someone took a little while. Of course, my aunt and uncle quickly found out what was going on. People told them I had been revving it up and spinning tires all over town. I had the car for less than an hour and I tore it up. Needless to say, I got my ass torn up, too.

By the time I got to high school a lot of changes were taking place in the local school systems. Two area schools, LaRose Cut Off and Golden Meadow, which had previously been longtime rivals, consolidated into South Lafourche High School. I attended the first two years of high school at LaRose Cut Off. They built a brand-new school, and I was in the first graduating class of South Lafourche High School. Students got to help select the new mascot and form new clubs. It was an exciting time for students!

And though things were changing, high school administrators, teachers, and even police were a lot more lenient on kids back then. Mistakes made at a tender age were not the end of your life in those days. Kids were not labeled and discarded for their shortcomings or harmless shenanigans. For instance, when I was in high school the legal drinking age was eighteen, but no one ever bothered to check IDs any way. There was a place right across from the high school called the Safari Club with live music, booze, and nothing but a bunch of high school kids having a good time! If you happened to get pulled over, the cops usually took you home instead of down to the station. Back then they just let your parents deal with kids. And back then, parents would! Back in those days, law enforcement didn't try to throw the book at you or taint your record for the rest of your life either. They seemed to recognize that we were just kids who wanted to have a good time, and that we were just trying to find our way to adulthood.

I liked clowning around in high school. I was always trying to be funny, and I usually was! I snuck around to smoke cigarettes with my friends. Their dads owned tugboats, and I ended up working for one of them during the summer breaks from college. They were always better off than we were, and they had a lot of cool stuff, so I made friends with them. One of the kids was a few years younger than me. He had an old go-kart with a 5.5 Briggs and Stratton engine, and he would ride us up and down the street. It was a blast! He also had a horse that he would let us take turns riding. We had a lot of fun together hunting, fishing, and playing sports.

I was a reporter for our high school newspaper, and I also participated in the business administration and the drama club. I really enjoyed drama club. I helped build sets and I enjoyed being part of the creative process. I took pride in creating a nice production. We performed Our Time, by Thornton Wilder, and I played the role of the town drunk. I also got to travel across the country to New York City and Washington D.C. on my senior class trip. It was great! We hopped on a tour bus at the high school and headed to the east coast. We took pictures in front of the White House and saw the Supremes at the Copa Cabana in New York. It was an incredible trip. High school was good for me. I enjoyed school but I was very shy with girls. I only had two dates in four years. One date was to Junior Prom and the other was to Senior Prom. We were typical teenagers. We partied, drank beer, and raised a little hell all along the way, but like my dates, high school ended mostly uneventful.

My cousin, Morris, was a local basketball star. We played a lot of basketball in our neighborhood, and in junior high I convinced Morris to try out for the basketball team with me. He made it and I didn't. I was able to find a place on an intramural team eventually, but they never let me play much because I wasn't a great ball handler. My team made it all the way to the league's intramural championship finals game. Someone fouled out, and I was the last man standing. Or rather, I was the last man sitting on the bench, so they had no choice but to put me in for the remaining 15 to 20 seconds. One of our guards threw up a shot in the final seconds and he missed. As the ball came down, I leapt into the air and tipped the ball into the net, and we won the game! By luck or accident, either way I'll take the win. It was the most exciting moment in sports I ever experienced. The buzzer went off as time ran out on the game, and we were the champions! I never played sports in school, but I gave them all hell in my neighborhood sporting events.

Just a few months before I graduated high school, I began to seriously consider my future and decided I wanted to go to college. My father had always hoped I would become a choir director, but there was no way in hell that was happening. I also knew Vietnam was upon us and my lottery number was 26, which practically guaranteed that I would be sent off to war. I got a college catalog. My father asked how I was going to pay for school, and I just told him I would find a way. I had two choices — Northwestern State University, or Nicholls State University, which was only about thirty miles away and locally referred to as Harvard on the Bayou. Knowing I would find a way, I went ahead and registered for college at Northwestern State University in Natchitoches, Louisiana (pronounced Nackatish). Natchitoches is the original French colony in Louisiana and is the oldest settlement in the Louisiana Purchase. Established in 1714, it is perhaps best known for being the film location for Steel Magnolias, the 1989 award winning dramedy. I didn't really have any particular reason to choose Northwestern, other than knowing a few people who planned to attend there in the fall. My neighbor Ronnie and some of my other church friends were registered there, and I figured it was far enough away from home that I could do whatever I wanted. I just had to come up with the cash to make it happen. I hadn't turned 18 yet and wouldn't until July 21. I would have to wait to go work offshore legally with the big boys. That's where the money was.

While I waited to turn 18, I took a job at a Ledet Brothers Grocery Store in Golden Meadow. I worked as a bag boy for one dollar an hour every day they would let me until my birthday. Jerry, the owner, was a character. He was a short, balding man, who always appeared half shaven, and he was a real cheapo. I remember watching him stretch a dollar with blood and fat to make more hamburger patties. He cut corners at every turn to save a dime. I once heard that he tried to bury a body in his yard to avoid funeral costs. The story goes, an old man that worked for him also lived in his shed in his back yard. Jerry found the old man dead one morning, and instead of calling the coroner, he just started digging a hole in the back yard. Supposedly, a neighbor happened by while out walking his dog and saw him digging the hole and asked what he was doing. He responded, "The old man died and he ain't got no money or anything, so I'm just going to bury him in the backyard." Of course, you can't do that. Not even cheapo Jerry could cut that corner.

The day before my birthday, I quit the grocery store, and by the next day I had a job as a deckhand on a crew boat stationed out of Dulac, Louisiana, about fifty miles away from my parents' house. The crew boat worked seven days on and seven days off, but I stayed out there forty days that summer before I went to college. I made twenty-one dollars per day as a deckhand on the crew boat. Every dime I made went towards my tuition, books, and housing. My mother also took a job as a cafeteria cook while I was in college so that she could send me fifty dollars every month.

I spent the rest of the summer working nonstop on that boat in the Gulf of Mexico until it was time to shove off for college. It was just me and the crew boat captain, who was one of my friend's dads. I was pulling in good money doing delivery work on a 60-foot steel hull cabin vessel. We transported welders, pipefitters, and other hands who worked offshore. We delivered mail, groceries, and basically anything anyone needed on the rigs. Right before the summer was ending, sometime in August 1967, Hurricane Beulah pushed inland nearby. We were servicing at that time and sending crews out to a pipeline barge, but due to the hurricane no one was making runs out to the rigs.

It was cloudy and rainy, and the seas were incredibly rough. We got a delivery call for a mail bag and a case of milk. The captain said we would give it a try, so we grabbed the necessary provisions they had requested and headed out of the main channel. Our vessel had two Caterpillar V-12 engines, and by the time we left the channel we were probably going about 35 knots. As soon as we breached the protection of the jetties we were at full speed. We went over the top of the first swell that met us, and the boat came down like a hundred tons of bricks. Water poured over the boat and anything that wasn't nailed down went flying into the air, including me and the captain! For the next two hours we battled those swells, accelerating over them and bottoming out over and over until we finally reached the barge. As the captain passed them the mail and milk, I heard him say, "Don't ever ask me to do this again. I'm not going out if it's that rough again." I don't know if he ever went out in that kind of weather again, but it scared the shit out of me, and I would not do it again.

The summer finally came to an end, and I had enough money to start college classes in the fall. I felt accomplished knowing that I could make something happen by working for it. If it hadn't been for that job, I would have never been able to go to college. And if it hadn't been for grit, determination, and the desire to have more, I could have easily ended up a long-term deckhand, who might have had aspirations of becoming a captain one day. But I was the master of my fate, and I knew it was time to move on from the Bayou Lafourche.

Chapter Four: Off to The Races

I could hardly wait to start college, and not because I was eager to expand my young mind, at least not through books and lectures. It was a matter of knowing I didn't want to go into the military, and that I was ready to get the hell out of Cut Off. I wanted to get away from my parents and start my own life without all the antiquated family influence. I picked the easiest major I could so that it wouldn't bog down my time with schoolwork, because that was not the point of college in my young mind. I couldn't pack my bags fast enough! My whole family loaded up in the car to bring me to Northwestern. It was a pretty big deal because I was the only Gordon who had ever gone away to college. My father had attended a few classes while in the Navy, but no one in my family really had a great education.

I ended up rooming with my longtime classmate and friend from church, Ronnie. Rooming with Ronnie also came with the added benefit that he had a car. He was an only child and his parents had recently purchased him a brand-new two-tone Pontiac Le Mans with a vinyl top. We all loaded up; Ronnie with his parents, and me and my "whole famdamily," and we took off to Natchitoches.

Natchitoches is about 300 miles from Cut Off, which took about six to seven hours by car. We left the bayou country and passed Baton Rouge, all the way up to LA 1, and then headed northwest, leaving the swampland behind. The closer I got to college, the more the terrain changed. By the time we reached Alexandria boggy bayous had given way to hills covered with pine trees. Alexandria is sort of like the Mason Dixon Line of Louisiana, and everything north of there, looks and feels a lot like the piney woods of East Texas. They say the bottom half of Louisiana is for Cajuns and Coonasses while the top half is filled with rednecks, which are typically East Texans. It is a great divide that has sliced through the state's culture. For instance, in northern Louisiana you're more likely to catch a Cowboys football game on in a sports bar than a Saints game. That's just pitiful.

Our parents helped us get settled on campus in the brand-new male dorm, Rapides Hall. We were on the top floor, and I was on top of the world! Back then there were no coed college dorms. Hell, women still had mandatory curfews in college at that time. I was a typical coonass, but I was smart enough to be glad I wasn't a woman because they had fewer rights. There was a set of bunkbeds and a small desk in our room. It was practically a closet. I couldn't have been happier to be moving out of my parents' house and into that closet.

As soon as our parents pulled out of the parking lot, we started mingling and meeting people. I met and made friends with a lot of guys from up north. There were a lot of people from Shreveport and Alexandria at Northwestern, but I made friends with the "Yankees," Charlie, Michael, who we called "Buggy," and Bob. The only reason they were at Northwestern was because they couldn't afford the fancy colleges in Boston, New York, or Connecticut. It was actually cheaper to pay out of state tuition and fees. They were basically foreigners in a strange new land, but truth be told, so was I. Southern Louisiana might as well have been Mexico in respect to the difference from north Louisiana. Everyone was fascinated with my accent. They had never met a Coonass, and they had never heard an accent like mine. Instead of saying "this and that," I said, "dis and dat." It was just natural for us to speak that way, and to be clear, I still speak a little Coonass, but not "fluently" anymore.

Coonasses just have a different and more colorful way of saying or explaining things. Over the years it became clear to me that Coonasses should probably stay out of marketing all together. When I was a kid there was a guy in Golden Meadow who owned a sanitation business called Ray Bouvier Sanitation. His slogan was, "Your shit is our bread and butter!" And over time, Coonass' marketing abilities did not improve. Much later in life, I returned home to take some of my buddies fishing. We needed some bait, so we stopped in at a bait shop called "Minnow Pause." I have no doubt the business venture and name had been the brainchild of a Coonass who had overheard a conversation about menopause and decided it was the perfect name for a bait shop. Leave it to a Coonass.

Ronnie and I quickly earned nicknames. I was a lot bigger and taller than him, so I became "Big Coon," and he became "Little Coon." Those nicknames stuck with us through the duration of college. It wasn't long at all before a fraternity had extended invitations to pledge during rush. I joined the Tau

45

Kappa Epsilon (TKE) fraternity my first semester of college. It's one of the largest collegiate men's social fraternities and is centered around advancing character and personal development. "A Teke is a man who is trustworthy and lives the values of helping each member integrate love, charity, and esteem in their daily lives." It was all mostly bullshit. The frat was full of Yankees and Jews. I was a coonass and didn't fit in. So, we were all outcasts together.

College wasn't necessarily hard, but my grades didn't reflect my level of intelligence by any means. I practically graduated with 'un-honors' because I never studied. I got mostly Cs and might have had an A in P.E. once. It was pitiful. But I did get my pilot license while I was at Northwestern. I never flew again after getting my license in college though.

My first two years of college were disorienting and reminded me of the story of Boudreaux's talking dog.

Boudreaux and Pierre were best friends. One day, Pierre decided to drop by Boudreaux's house, where he saw a sign on the fence that read, Talking Dog for Sale. Behind the fence Pierre saw a beautiful Labrador retriever. Pierre asked the Labrador, "Are you the talking dog?"

Much to his surprise the Labrador says, "Oui oui, that's me."

Pierre was stunned and said, "Oh my goodness, how did this happen?"

The Labrador explained that he had the gift of speech since he was a puppy. The Labrador told Pierre that he joined the circus, but the people didn't treat him very well, so he ran away. He told Pierre he joined the CIA next, thinking he could help them out, but he explained that he got homesick and decided to return to Lafayette where he became a police dog and helped them sniff out drugs. The Labrador said he had retired just about a year ago, when Boudreaux walked up.

Boudreaux asked Pierre, "Whatchu tink?"

Pierre was astounded and asked how much Boudreaux wanted for the talking dog. Boudreaux thought for a second and said he would take ten dollars. Pierre was shocked, "Ten dollars? Wow, that's so cheap?!"

Boudreaux said, "Yeah, but everything he tells you is a lie." In Cajun, that's called "Focusin' on da wrong ting."

I had obviously focused on the wrong things my first two years of college, but I had a hell of a good time in my fraternity! I met some great guys there, and almost immediately my whole life became about the fraternity. Monobrow Charlie from Boston, Bob from Connecticut, and Buggy, a short Italian Jewish guy with long, black, curly hair were among my first brothers.

Looking back on my time with TKE, it reminds me a lot of the 1978 movie, *Animal House,* starring John Belushi. It was

47

wild and we had a lot of fun! The fraternity kept us connected on the weekends when everyone disappeared. Most students went home to Alexandria or Shreveport on the weekends because there wasn't much to do at Northwestern. By Friday afternoon everyone who wasn't in a frat was pulling out of town. If you weren't leaving for the weekend or part of a fraternity, you were screwed because there was absolutely nothing to do.

Hazing was part of pledging. No one beat anyone's ass, and I never witnessed anything over the top or dangerous, but there was some paddling. Other than that, they might ask you to do something weird like wake up at 1 a.m. and go do their laundry. Getting accepted into the fraternity wasn't hard. At the end of pledge there was a big ceremony, during which they revealed all their secret ways, handshakes, and public phrases to the new pledges. And once you performed, you conformed. I've never considered myself to be a conformist. I have always hated exclusion because I was always excluded during my childhood. I was excluded from the pretty people, the jocks, and the rich kids. Everyone had a clique, but mine had always been the impoverished one, and I desperately didn't want to be included in that one anymore. The TKE's gave me a sense of belonging. I was immediately part of something bigger and better than what I ever had been. I had moved up the ladder of life in a way that I had earned on my own, and it felt good to pull myself up the ranks of life. Education gave me the first chance to better myself, and I did, despite what my pathetic GPA said.

The parish wasn't dry, but Natchitoches only had two liquor stores, alcohol was not served in restaurants, and there were no bars. You couldn't sit at a bar and order a drink, but you could swing by a drive through window and order whatever you wanted. The cheapest thing to drink was wine. Back then you could get a pint of red wine, either red ripple or red Tokay for about eighty-five cents. Beer was the next cheapest thing to drink. Whatever you drank in college depended on your pocketbook and maybe your mood.

We had no transportation to get to either of the liquor stores. The only other place to find a drink was to go all the way across town on Old Gandicor Road, to the edge of the city limits. There, at the edge of town, was a pizza joint owned by a sharp but shrewd and nerdy entrepreneur. He had horseshoe baldness and a pot belly, but he was a super personable guy. He took a shine to us for whatever reason. Maybe he liked my accent, maybe he liked the Yankees, or maybe he was just entertained by our ignorance. Who knows, but he was always nice to us, and I was glad to know him. We were stuck in Natchitoches every weekend with no place to go except his pizza joint, where he let us drink pitchers of beer until we puked. Every weekend we would catch a ride with someone to the edge of town and that is what we did— ate pizza and drank beer until we puked.

I made it through the first semester of beer and pizza, and the next semester I became the Vice President of Northwestern's TKE chapter. I had quickly moved up in rank and was living the high life. But life got even higher when I ditched the V.P. role and became the social chairman! That role was responsible for arranging all the fun stuff. I was a damn good social chairman. I had events planned every week, most of which involved alcohol.

49

We had killer keg parties in the woods. Even though I had moved up north, we were still in the South. We would buy a keg of beer and hike out into the woods to find a good spot and get it all set up for the party. It didn't take long to get the head off it and get the party going. We'd drink all night, and the next day, as soon as the hangover would allow, we returned for cleanup. No one picked up trash back then. My god, it was embarrassing. When I think back to that era and how people disrespected the earth so much by just throwing their crap all over the place, I am disgusted.

My outcast friends and I did a lot of cool stuff in college. Once we even started a business. I met this guy who had been playing football at Texas A & M University in College Station. He had a James Bond car and we thought he seemed cool. My friends and I got to know him, and we all came up with a plan to start a TV guide. We sold ads to businesses in town— hardware stores, grocery stores, restaurants, it didn't matter what kind of business it was. We knocked on doors and beat the street. But in college when you start something you are running on fumes from the very beginning. The TV Guide just got to be too much and flopped about two months in. Live and learn.

It didn't take long before my buddies and I had concocted another brilliant plan. We decided we could make some big money by throwing a concert and dance. We arranged for Question Mark and the Mysterion, the artists responsible for the hit song 96 Tears, to play in Alexandria. We all chipped in to pay their booking fees and rented a venue. I chipped in all the money I had, including the money I had saved for my spring tuition. I believed this business venture was going to bankroll me for a while. As luck would have it, the weekend we scheduled the dance for was also the weekend that Gone with the Wind was rereleased at drive-ins. It totally killed our sales. I lost all my money and had to borrow money for the spring semester.

I wasn't afraid to work or take risks. Later these two elements would prove to be my demise in so many ways and my saving grace in others. Having the balls to do something and having the sense not to do something are two drastically different things, but the line was often skewed or hard to find. I had the balls for sure, but good sense came much later. But when you're young, you don't know how stupid you are. In fact, when you're young you're so stupid that you think you are the smartest person you know.

When my first year of school was over, I returned to Cut Off to work on the tugboat. I worked every summer on the Gulf so I could pay for college. My second summer in the oil field, I stayed out on the tugboat the full ninety days, dragging oil rigs in the Gulf and through the bayous, and pushing barges around for about twenty-eight dollars a day. The tugboats were huge, about eighty feet long, with three-story cabins. Our crew consisted of the captain, a shipmate and three deckhands. The captain's shift was from 7 a.m. until 7 p.m. The shipmate got the shit jobs and the graveyard shift. The cabin cannot be empty, therefore one deckhand remained in the cabin with the captain or shipmate. In the movies you often see crews painting or constantly chipping on the vessel, but those chores only happen

51

if the boat is anchored, not moving, and there isn't anything else to do. And when that happened, it was complete misery.

One time we got a call to pull a deep-water rig from south Houston to the mouth of the mighty Mississippi. Deep water rigs never sit on the ocean floor. Rather, they have a ballast tank that makes it buoyant, and acts as a big storage tank that pumps water in and out as needed. The cables on this rig were thicker than coffee cans, and the anchors were huge. When we arrived, there were flags and buoys indicating where the rig should be placed. The setup process was lengthy and tedious. The massive cables and anchors were dragged out in all different directions and operated by wenches. Then the barge began to pump water into the tank to get the rig in the right place and position. Once positioned correctly, all the water was pumped out of the tank causing the rig to pull against the anchors and secure it. The engineering behind this setup was impressive.

That summer on the tugboat was epic. I met a lot of cool people and formed some great friendships, which was good because I basically lived with those people and there was nothing else to do. We were floating out on the water with no television, we couldn't pick up a radio station, and eight tracks were still so new no one really had one. This was still during the days of reel-to-reel, but who the hell had one of those handy? It was great to strike up friendships with the crew to pass the time. The next two summers I worked as a welder's assistant for a company called Bill Dixon's Welding, which contracted through Chevron.

When you're out that far in the Gulf of Mexico, about twenty-five to thirty miles offshore, the water is blue and beautiful. The waters and coastlines of Louisiana and Texas look nothing like the shorelines of Florida or even Alabama. Down here, when we watch the waves lap against the shore it looks a little more like mud lapping onto the shore most of the year. One day while we were transporting the deep-water rig, I was standing in the wheelhouse, and I'll never forget what a beautiful sight I witnessed. The sky was bright blue and cloudless, and it seemed to merge with the glassy blue waters we were gliding against. The water was so still it looked slick. In the distance, but not far, I could see a school of tarpons breaching the blue waters. The silver kings seemed to fly out of the ocean and flop in the air before plunging back down into the sea. We were only able to pull the deep-water rig about three miles per hour, so we didn't disturb the tarpons or the water. It was one of the most beautiful sights I've ever witnessed.

But it wasn't all beautiful sunsets and blue waters in the Gulf of Mexico. There were days when I wondered why in the hell I even bothered. On one occasion, I was in the shower and there was very little water pressure. I was put out about the pressure but carried on about my business. Suddenly, blood and guts exploded from the faucet onto my face. A mouse carcass had been lodged in the pipes and in that moment, there was finally enough pressure built up behind him to force him out. Mind you, I showered every day and brushed my teeth at least twice a day with that water. In the moment that rat bastard exploded on me, I sincerely questioned if that job was worth it in that moment.

53

When my ninety days were up that second summer, I came back to shore with a pocket full of money. My dad located a car for me to buy— a 1962 Chevy Nova that had previously been owned by a carpenter. I paid $600 for it with my own money, and no financial help from my parents. The car was about six years old, but it was new to me. It was a two-door coupe with a six-cylinder engine, which gave it some cool clout, or at least I thought it did. It was factory blue with a white top. I thought I had died and gone to heaven! I loved that car. I didn't care that it wasn't brand new. Hell, I didn't even care that it had a hole rusted through the floorboard right by the accelerator pedal. I cut a small piece of tin and placed it behind the thick vinyl floor mat so I wouldn't see the highway as I went on down the road.

I hopped in my Chevy Nova and headed back to Northwestern after a long summer of good, hard work. My friends and I had already decided not to live in the dorms when we returned for the fall semester. I moved off campus with my fraternity brothers and into a quadraplex on Jefferson Street near campus. There were two doors on the bottom and a hallway leading upstairs to the top two apartments. We had the bottom right apartment with a huge living room. There was plenty of room for everyone. Well, except for my fraternity brother Jim, who probably weighed about 350 pounds.

My fraternity brothers were my life and family. My brother, Jimmy, showed back up to school in a 1962 Rambler with chrome mags that year. We both loved music. We had eight track players in our cars, and we blared our music everywhere we went. We had this Four Tops thing we did, and we thought we were so cool. Hell, we were cool! His girlfriend was still in high school, but he was crazy about her. Every Friday he would pack up and head home to Opelousas to spend time with her. His dad finally put a stop to those weekend warrior trips because it cost too much to run back and forth, and he felt it was a distraction to Jimmy. His dad told him he could only leave school once a month to see his girlfriend. We came up with a plan to get him back to his sweetheart more often than that.

Jimmy and I decided to switch cars so he could travel back to Opelousas undetected by his parents. This was long before the days of cell phones and being able to track teenagers, college students, or anyone for that matter. Once you left someone's sight, you were gone. I rode around Natchitoches in his car all weekend. It was great! But Jimmy didn't cruise down to Opelousas to see his girlfriend like we had planned. When he got to Opelousas the muffler fell off my car. He had to take it to the muffler shop, and while he was there his dad happened to drive by and busted him. Jimmy came back so pissed off. I couldn't help but laugh, but he didn't think it was as funny as I did.

Jimmy never did learn his lesson about loaning his cars to me. Later he loaned me the new Oldsmobile Cutlass his dad had just bought for him on the weekend of the Louisiana State Fair. The State Fair was a big deal, and everyone went. This time around I was taking the hottest woman I'd ever laid eyes on to the State Fair— Sheila. To this day I wonder how in the hell I got that woman to go on a date with me, but I did, and I will never forget it. And I bet she won't either.

We were running a little behind on the way to the game. I was hauling ass in Jimmy's brand spanking new Cutlass to get to the fairgrounds off Interstate 20. Traffic was all backed up in front of my exit, but the right lane was empty, so I tore ass down the empty lane. I got about twenty yards from the stop sign and a woman walked out in front of me. It scared the shit out of me, and I cut the wheel hard to the right and slammed on the brakes. I heard a thump and looked in the rearview mirror where I saw a lady laying on the ground. My date and I jumped out of the car and rushed over to her. I asked her if she was hurt but she said she was fine, and she did seem fine. Traffic was really starting to back up because I had the road blocked. The lady walked off and left with no complaints or problems. There was no damage to the car, so my hot date resumed. I figured Jimmy would never find out what had happened in his new car. About two years later while I was in the service in Germany, I got a summons to appear in court for a hit and run. Needless to say, Jimmy found out. The woman who had stepped out in front of the car had decided to sue. His dad owned the car, so he was also being sued. The trial was postponed until I got home from Germany. I was practically delighted when I saw Sheila walk into the courtroom. She was married to some hotshot by then, but she looked like a Playboy model when she took the stand. I watched her ascend to the stand, and in that moment, I was glad I was there to see her, even if it meant I was being sued for a hit and run! Sheila and I both just told the truth and we won. Jimmy went on to get elected to the Supreme Court of Louisiana in 2017, despite his questionable judgement in loaning out his vehicle.

Another fraternity brother of mine that I'll never forget was Sam. He had a buddy named Freddy that he hung out with a lot. Sam looked like Jug Head from the comic book. He was skinny with a big head, and a huge Adam's apple. Freddy was about that good looking, too. They didn't have much luck getting dates, but they finally managed to hook up with some girls who lived in the dorms. The girls were also about as attractive as the guys, so it was a pretty good match. Sam picked the girls up in his 1954 Chevrolet his dad had given him. It was in pristine condition until that night. Sam and Freddy managed to get laid that night. Unfortunately, they didn't quite make it home with the girls, and I do not believe there were any second dates to follow. Sam's date, Phyllis, was sitting by him in the middle of the bench seat, when he had to hit the brakes, causing her face to collide with the metal dashboard. There was absolutely no padding or soft surface on the dash in that year model. Her mouth hit the dash so hard that it chipped the paint off and knocked her two front teeth out. The ding in the dash was pretty bad, but Phyllis needed medical attention. Sam and Freddy took the girls to the hospital, dropped them off with two less teeth, and never looked back. Turned out, Phyllis's dad was a State Trooper, and he was pissed about the whole incident. James's car wasn't hard to find, so the trooper found him, and he got in big trouble. We all thought he was going to jail, but he didn't. We never saw "Flying Phyllis" again, but we will never forget the night she flew into the dash.

More than Phyllis had been flying. Time was passing so quickly, and I had finally met a girl. I had never been in a relationship before. Until then, I had still only ever been on two dates. But as college was winding down, finding someone to settle down with seemed like the natural order of what I should do next. So, I basically married the first girl who smiled at me. One night my buddy was on the phone with a bunch of girls, and they were flirting and going back and forth. I got pulled into the conversation, and that's how I met my first wife, Linda. She was cute, she had an MGA Coupe, and her parents had a pool in the back yard. They appeared loaded in my eyes. I didn't have shit back then. My pool was the bayou. I was 21 and she was 22. She was from Fort Worth, Texas and I was from Cut Off, Louisiana. I had never even been laid! We dated but never got along famously, although we did bond over our newfound Bahai faith. I took her to the spring fraternity ball; I was the president, and she was the queen. By September, just before rush, we decided to get married, and I couldn't even afford a ring. If it had not been for my friend Jim, I don't know what I would have given Linda as a symbol of my love, for whatever that was worth. Jim gave me a rose cut diamond from his own mother's ring. He had it taken out and set on a band for me. I was lucky to have Jim in my life for so many reasons, but his ability to be so generous was always above and beyond. I'll always be grateful to him.

And just as fast as I had made my life and family with the fraternity, I ditched it because I was not willing to cut my hair and decided to marry Linda our senior year of college. We went to Shreveport and got married at the Captain Shreveport Hotel like hippies, complete with a Bahai ceremony. I had long sandy blonde hair and wore a stark white suite and shiny white shoes. But regardless of what religion we married under, or just how sharp I looked at the wedding, our marriage was doomed from the beginning. Sometimes it takes a while to figure out you've made a mistake, and sometimes it takes even longer to admit your mistake, but by day one of our honeymoon it was over for me.

We honeymooned in Galveston, where we stayed at the Flagship Hotel. Linda and I rented a moped to cruise around on the island, and as we rode down the Seawall and her arms wrapped around me, I thought to myself, "What the fuck have I done?" When the honeymoon ended, we returned to school in Natchitoches. We were broke as hell and needed a place to live. My friend Jim and all my other fraternity brothers who had lived in the quadraplex were graduating, so I got the entire apartment and we moved in to start our new lives. I graduated with a degree, just barely, and Linda put her education on hold. We were off to a shitty start.

Chapter Five Losing My Religion

"That's me in the corner
That's me in the spotlight
Losing my religion
Trying to keep up with you
And I don't know if I can do it
Oh no, I've said too much
I haven't said enough"

— *REM Losing My Religion*

My father was a demanding and devout Southern Baptist. He demanded that we be in church every time the doors were open. He felt his family should appear to be a model Southern Baptist family, even if he wasn't. We Gordons, who couldn't be Catholic, spent most of our lives marching through church doors, attending revivals and gospel singings, and singing in the choir, all to make my father happy. He had great hopes that I would become a choir director one day, but it never took. That was the absolute last thing in the world I wanted to do with my life. The only reason I was even in the choir was because I thought singing was the only fun thing about church.

I have to joke about it sometimes, but church did not edify me whatsoever. I knew a lot about church, maybe even more than I wanted to. I certainly knew more than the three Coonasses who tried to get into Heaven.

Three Coonasses were killed in an automobile accident. As they approached the pearly gates, St. Peter was standing there. He scanned through his book, then turned to them and said, "Man, I can't let any of ya'll in here. Ya'll don't know anything about God or religion, and I can't just let you into Heaven. But I'll tell y'all what, if any of you can tell me the Christmas story, I'll let all three of you in."

The first Coonass jumped up eagerly and said, "I know what it is! It's dat one time of year when little kids put on scary costumes and knock on people's door for candy. Everybody have a good time, and dat is the Christmas Story."

"No, that's Halloween," said St. Peter.

The second Coonass piped up and said he knew the Christmas story. "It's that time of year where you get all your family together, cook a turkey and eat pie. Everybody have a good time, and dat is the Christmas Story."

"No, that's Thanksgiving," said St. Peter.

The last Coonass said, "I tink I know what dat is. Once upon a time in a faraway land, there was a baby child born in a barn with some chickens and some goats. There were three wise guys who owned some camels. They was out riding one night and having a good time, and they kept seeing a big bright star stuck in the sky. They didn't know what it was so they decided to see if they could run it down. They rode towards the star and found a baby in a barn. They thought he was very cute; so they gave him some presents for his birthday. Later on, that little boy grew up to be real smart, and the people who ran their country were concerned that he might take over. So, what they did was, they nailed him to a cross, they killed him and buried him."

St. Peter was astonished. He said, "I can't believe you know the Christmas Story."

The Coonass said, "No, no. Dat story not finished yet. Three days later, somehow that guy came back to life. He got out of his grave and saw his own shadow, and POOF! There were six more weeks of winter."

There was a certain way you were expected to behave in church, and if that line was crossed even my mother would throw you under the bus— the bus being my father's iron fist, with which he ruled his household. Our pastor wasn't particularly fond of me because I was known to talk in church. He would warn the other boys about behaving like me. "Don't be like James," he would say. When I was about fourteen, during a guest preacher's sermon, I crossed the line. I was sitting in the back of the sanctuary with my buddies, and we were yapping and

63

picking at each other, like typical teenage boys. Our pastor left the sanctuary and reentered through the front door, behind where my buddies and I were sitting. He tapped us on the shoulder and told us to behave. My mother was mortified! When we got to the dinner table that evening, she said, "Jimmy, why don't you tell your father what happened at church?" My heart sank. My mother had just served me up to the grizzly bear sitting next to me at the dinner table, who hadn't even been at church.

She made me tell my father that I had misbehaved in church and that the pastor reprimanded me. When I told him the pastor had gotten up and lightly tapped my shoulder and told me to be quiet, he calmly sat his fork down then he hit me so hard that I fell out of my chair and to the ground. The Southern Baptist pastor's reprimand paled in comparison to my father's. Knocking me out of my chair wasn't enough. After all, I had committed an egregious error; I had talked in church and needed to be taught a lesson. He stood up from the table and put his foot on the back of my head, pushing my face against the linoleum, causing blood to gush from my nose. It was everywhere and dinner was ruined, all because I giggled with my buddies on the pew at church.

Oddly enough, once I left home my father never attended church again. His best friend was a mausoleum salesman, and he was known to be a drinker. The pastor declined to let my father's drinking buddy collect the offering at church and told him it was because he drank too much. This did not sit well with my father, perhaps because he was known to drink more than his fair share. He confronted the pastor and never darkened the door again, because he felt his friend had been wronged. The truth probably has more to do with self-realization than defending anyone's reputation and right to collect offering at a church.

Imagine my surprise when I came home from college to find out mom and dad no longer attended church because his drinking buddy was not allowed to collect the offering. After all those years of forcing us into the pews, he left the church over another man's reputation who wasn't even family. I had long since resented being forced into church, and every religious event that was within driving distance, but when my parents suddenly stopped going after forcing us to go for all those years, it left a bad taste in my mouth. Worse yet, it was always rumored that the pastor had made inappropriate passes and advances at several young girls in the community. Those whispers went on for years, but as far as I know, no one cared enough to actually look into it.

My experience in the Southern Baptist Church forever shaped my view of religion and the people who practiced it in my life. I hated the hypocrisy and the double standards of my father based on his ideas of church and religion for his family. He treated us like shit while setting ridiculous standards, of which he himself did not abide. If you couldn't live up to his standards, then you couldn't be in his world—a world that only existed in his mind. Church tore at the fabric of my family, and often seemed to make a bad situation worse. When I turned eighteen, I was finally able to make my own decisions regarding religion— and I did. I left and never went back. I felt like I had been to church enough in my lifetime at that point. All these years later, and I still feel the same.

College is a time of discovery. Most of our lives are lived in discovery mode, but when we reach college age, we begin to make our own discoveries independently from everyone who, up until that point, has dictated what you would do in your day-to-day life. During my first year of college at Northwestern, my friend Jim introduced me to a new kind of religion called Bahá'í. I was so sick of religion as I had known it. I respected Jim and I was generally an openminded person. He was cool and this was far different from any kind of religion I had ever known or been exposed to. The Bahá'í faith appeared to be the exact opposite of the Southern Baptist doctrine, so I went with it. Why the hell not? The Bahá'í practiced and believed things I didn't even realize people considered religion. They believed in the inherent nobility of human beings, the fundamental equality of the sexes, harmony between religion and science, justice among all human endeavors, the vital role of education and advancing towards collective maturity. Like I said, why the hell not, but later Bahá'í saved my ass.

Linda and I had a Bahá'í wedding ceremony, which I am sure both crushed and embarrassed my parents, on top of me being a longhaired hippie in a white wedding suit. That was just a bonus as far as I was concerned. The cherry on top—if you will. I endured years of their church, so they could endure my wedding day.

While I was in college, I also discovered marijuana. It was love at first toke. In fact, the first time I smoked marijuana I said, "I am going to smoke this shit for the rest of my life." I've made good on that pledge most of the years that have followed, although there were a few years that I didn't partake. In the time that it takes to smoke a joint with friends, I knew that marijuana was going to be part of my life for the long haul.

After barely sliding by and graduating with a degree in business administration, Linda and I moved to Fort Worth. We lived with her parents while I started working at Thom McAn Shoes. Her parents hated me. Her mother especially hated me. Everything I did bothered that woman. If I blew my nose, it was the end of the world to her. She hated me with every fiber of her being and I felt every bit of it. It was palpable. We moved out just as soon as we could, but as luck or fate would have it, I was drafted just a few months later in 1971. We had just tied the knot and moved to Texas and knew this was coming. My lottery number, 26, basically ensured that I was going to Vietnam, or so I thought. Believing that, I quit my job in shoe sales and went to take my physical exam. I had been working as a manager trainee and the company had just approached me about taking an assistant manager position in Mesquite. That was what my life was shaping up to look like—a shoes salesman. Upon reporting for duty at the Dallas AAFES station, I was ushered in with about forty other guys. After we passed our physicals, the group was given two options. The first was to go home and start our assignment sometime after the holidays when we received a letter, and the second was to start immediately. Well, I had already quit my job, and knowing I made a monumental mistake with my new bride, I felt I should start my two-year hitch right away.

It is incredible that one decision can change your life forever. Perhaps even more incredible is the fact that we make multiple lifechanging decisions throughout our lives, often on a whim or not realizing that decision has the potential to turn a world upside down. I could never have expected that just days after I reported for duty and turned down the opportunity to go home and start later, that headlines would ring out that the draft had ended. Those who had not started their service no longer had to report for duty at all. And there I was, already enlisted and brand new to basic training. Had I waited to start until after the holidays, my entire life probably would have been different. I do not recall being disappointed, but I think that had more to do with my brand-new marriage.

They shipped us out to Fort Polk in Louisiana, where they shaved our heads and gave us our gear and a duffle bag to put it in. Fort Polk's terrain was very similar to Vietnam, making it a perfect location for troops to prepare for what seemed inevitable.

Because I was a registered Bahá'í, I was able to transfer and become a conscientious cooperator. My faith, at the time, prevented me from carrying weapons, but it also propelled me into healthcare. I was immediately shipped to Fort Sam Houston, near San Antonio, to do twelve weeks of basic training. After basic, I began medic training. Medics were highly likely to be sent to Vietnam. We were required to do all the same workout routines as everyone else, but without carrying or using weapons. I am not saying I couldn't have done it, because I believe it wouldn't have taken long for me to pick up a weapon and start shooting back. All the same, I'm glad I didn't have to.

We arrived at nighttime, and they threw us in bunkbeds. By the next morning, we were playing Army. Every morning they woke us up harshly and started kicking us around, yelling and running us here and there. We jumped out of bed to put on pants, boots, and white t-shirts and fell into formation to run a mile first thing. Every day was the same. Before we brushed our teeth or anything else, we ran a mile. After the mile, we went to chow, where you had limited time to get in and get out. If you didn't get to eat that was just your tough shit. Basic was intense! You don't know physical hell unless you've been through basic training. When you think you can't go anymore, the Army somehow gets more out of you. They kick and push you all the way. I was 203 pounds when I started basic training. I had been in college and earned a beer gut. I was a physical wreck. It was the middle of winter and freezing, and those twelve weeks seemed to drag on forever. It was miserable. One time at the beginning, they asked for anyone with a college education to raise their hands, and I stupidly threw my hand up in the air. They put me on latrine duty. It was total bullshit. They broke us down as low as they could. Time went by, and every time I couldn't do twenty-five pushups, they made me do fifty. By the end of basic training, I passed the final physical fitness test with a 99, and I was a lean 165 pounds. That's what the Army does to you. When you finish basic training, you're the best man, physically, that you can be.

Most of the people doing basic training at Fort Sam Houston were conscientious cooperators. Lots of them were Seventh Day Adventists, but almost all of them claimed to be vegetarians. Nevertheless, almost every one of those vegetarians made an exception on steak night. I would tease them and say, "Y'all are strong in your convictions but willing to suffer a steak night for your country." There were a lot of great guys in basic, and I made good friends with three of them. Dave, from Rome, New York was probably my biggest buddy, but I was also close to Charlie, who had spent two years in the Peace Corps with his wife and had been drafted. We stuck together through basic and special training. We spent evenings in the rec room playing pool and listening to the jukebox. We were able to go to the PX and pick up new stuff, but we loved to pick up new music. We got the new Led Zeppelin and Pink Floyd, but we also got Elton John's Mad Man Across the Water. We played Tiny Dancer over and over while we played pool.

While we were in advanced individual training, we had to maintain a bunk on post that was made up for inspection, but we were allowed to live off post. So, the three of us got together and rented a little cottage close to the base at the Bungalow Apartments in San Antonio. It was great because we could go home and smoke pot and hang out.

We did Blue Cheer micro dot acid one weekend. My friends and I went to the Japanese Tea Gardens to enjoy the view and nature while we tripped. There was a gazebo at the top where the tramway was located. Everything was going great until some lady showed up and started talking to one of my buddies about some preacher on the radio that she liked to listen to. She went on to tell us how the preacher heard a knock on the door of his trailer one night, and it was a beautiful woman who needed assistance. She said the lady kept trying to make her way inside with him, but he wouldn't let her in because he knew she was really the devil disguised as a beautiful woman. I started to smile when she got to the part about the lady turning into the devil and challenging the preacher at the door. She looked at me and said, "You don't believe a word I'm saying, do you?"

I politely told her, "No, ma'am."

She moved on but it was a weird moment.

Radio preachers fighting beautiful shapeshifting women from their trailers would have amused me without the Blue Cheer.

Not every trip was that bizarre. When we dropped acid, we mostly listened to Led Zeppelin, and ate tacos from the park. Sometimes we rented bikes to ride to the botanical gardens. We had a lot of fun right up until we all went our separate ways.

Graduation day arrived and everyone got their orders. There were four companies with about one hundred men in each. I was in Charlie Company. Being in Charlie Company was the luckiest thing that had happened to me in a while, if not ever up to that point. When we were drafted, everyone filled out a dream sheet. We were told to list our top three choices for deployment.

No one chose Nam of course. Alpha, Bravo and Delta got their orders to go to Vietnam. They didn't get to go home and kiss their mamas goodbye. They were loaded up immediately and flown to San Diego and then on to Nam. Everyone in Charlie Company got their number one choice out of the three we were asked to list. I had listed Germany, Japan, and Hawaii as my top three destinations. Charlie also got Germany, and Dave got Hawaii. If we had all known each other sooner, we would have picked the same place. Charlie and I did do a little traveling together in Germany in his micro camping van, but my life went a different way and we got disconnected.

Since I wasn't being deployed to Vietnam, I went home for a week to see my wife. We had not been getting along and had mostly lived separate up to that point. I decided to give our marriage another shot and asked Linda, and our poodle named Maurice, to come to Germany with me. Almost as soon as I had gotten home it was time to leave again. This time I was to report to Fort Dix in New Jersey, where I would leave for Germany.

Chapter Six: Hash on Hand

I told Linda I would send for her when I got settled in Germany. Charlie and I arrived at Fort Dix, New Jersey, where my buddies from basic and I said our goodbyes. The next day, we all got on different planes, knowing most of us would never see each other again. Cheers to my buddies who got me through basic!

I can't recall much about the flight other than being in uniform with my gear and being packed in the plane like sardines. When we finally arrived, we disembarked and took a bus to a place that looked like a castle in the middle of the city, complete with brick wall fences and barbed wire. It was a dispatching area that the military had confiscated after World War II. We stayed there one night waiting for our assignments. While we waited, I took note of the countryside. It was so green that it commanded my attention. I never knew anything could be so lush and green. The next day, we lined up to receive our instruction. We waited in a line to speak with several army clerks at a table. There was a huge map of Europe behind them with special areas marked such as "First Cavalry," "First Infantry Division" and "TASCOM." I asked what TASCOM was, and the specialist replied, "That's Theatre Army support Command, like the USO, you entertain the troops."

I said, "That's what I want!" That sounded far enough away from tanks and artillery, and that was good enough for me. I couldn't have been luckier.

As a medical corpsman, I was assigned to the field hospital as a permanent duty station. It was eight-hour shift work for 40 hours a week with a lot of flexibility. I often worked 10 eight-hour days so I could take off every other Friday, Saturday, Sunday, and Monday to travel. I had never really considered working in a hospital and had landed in labor and delivery with a nerd, and typical Army sergeant named Jerry. We were responsible for 'catching the babies,' (hospital term for pulling them out of the mother), getting them cleaned up, giving them a vitamin K injection, and applying silver nitrate to their eyes before presenting them to the mother. There were only two American captains who were doctors. The Army had paid for them to go to medical school because there was a shortage of physicians in the military. They were basically doing time to pay off their educations. They hired German and Czech doctors to help with deliveries. We did about 70 deliveries a month. Overall, it was a great job. It was indoors and we had a lot of fun. There were a lot of hot, single American civilian nurses working there. They stayed on the BOQ in cheap apartments and traveled every weekend and any time off they had. There was one nurse in particular I was really attracted to, but despite my best efforts she didn't go for it. I was a jackass and would have been more than willing to cheat on my wife at that point.

I stayed in the Billets for a few months, where servicemen lived next door to the hospital, until Linda joined me in Germany. It didn't take me long to figure out that stereo and camera equipment were American soldiers' favorite hobbies. Most of them had thousands of dollars worth of equipment. All that kind of equipment was so cheap over there that everyone got into it. When Linda came over, I had to find an apartment for us. All I could afford was an apartment in the middle of a corn field that had been fertilized with hog shit. It was a tiny apartment with one small bedroom, a little living room, and a tiny kitchenette with a small fridge which forced us to buy groceries on a daily basis. Every piece of our furniture was used and often discarded by those leaving Germany heading back for the states. We would find cheap furniture and tie it to the hood of the car and haul it out to the corn field apartment. We were as broke in Germany as we were in America, but on a clear day you could see the Bavarian Alps from our apartment, and that somehow soothed me.

I was making $288 a month when I was first drafted. While I worked for the Army in Germany as a private first class, I made $320 per month. We barely scraped by and never had a damn dime left at the end of the month. But I didn't come all the way to Germany not to see Europe, so I came up with ways to make extra cash. At the first of every month, I would go to a Class Six store and buy up all the whiskey rations I could, about eight gallons, then I would go to the commissary and buy ten cartons of cigarettes. I would then sell all of our rations and the smokes for double what I had paid on base to the Labor and Delivery maid, Olga. That gave us a little extra money, but not enough to enjoy Europe.

I was so sick of being broke that I decided it was time to start dealing hash. It was pretty wide open back then, and there was no drug testing. A lot of good people left Germany as heroin addicts with Hepatitis B because it was too easy to go down that path. The Army barracks were basically a hash den. At 5 p.m. when the brass left, it was just a bunch of guys smoking hash and hanging out. During my time in Germany, I never saw marijuana, only hash. It only took me one day to find hash. The sergeant had retired for the evening, and the party had started. Everyone was listening to music, playing pool or foosball, smoking hash or shooting heroin. It was a zoo in there, so I jumped right in!

I got a few guys to go in together to buy some hash. I didn't have the money to buy as much as I needed to sell on my own. On the first attempt, we each put in $200 and tried to score, but we got ripped off. I had to find a better connection to get my business off the ground, and I had to do it myself because no one would invest money in drugs with me after we got screwed over. I started scoping out the Königsplatz, or the center of downtown Augsburg, where the street cars traverse. Germany had a great public transportation system, and the area was teeming with every walk of life. I wasn't sure who I was looking for initially, but as soon as I spotted him in the crowd, I knew he was my guy. There, in the middle of the Königsplatz, stood an unusually tall German guy who looked like he had just walked out of a rock concert. He had long black hair down his back, he was dressed in a stylish fur collar jacket with flaring blue jeans, and he was wearing KISS platform shoes that made him appear to be about 7'5" tall. It was like looking at a giant. He towered over the crowd and stood out like a sore thumb. I walked up to him and said, "Hey, man. What's going on?" He told me his name was Lossa, and just like that, I had made a new friend.

Lossa was the most stable hash connection I had. He brought his hash in from Holland and it was always good. We did a lot of business, but sometimes we just hung out. He lived in an apartment out in the middle of nowhere. Lossa moved so much hash that he had lookouts. He positioned two people at the road entries with walkie-talkies in case the police showed up, and he never kept the hash in his own apartment. Lossa moved about forty kilos of hash each month through a finely tuned distribution system. I could buy a kilo of hash, or about 1,000 grams, from Lossa for $1,000. I bought it for $1 per gram and sold it for $2 per gram, doubling my money. A thousand extra dollars, plus what I made selling my rations was pretty damn good money. My operation was smalltime compared to the volume Lossa did, but it made me feel like a big shot as I raked in travel and spending money.

When it was payday for the Army it was also my biggest payday for hash sales. The Army set up payday like an assembly line. You walked in and went to the first table where you picked up your check, signed it, and gave them your social security number. Then you walked to the next table, cashed your check, and proceeded out of the back door with your cash in hand. The Army didn't know it, but the next step in the assembly line was my business, on the other side of the back door, at the end of the payroll line. I always made sure I was the first person to get paid; then I would get into position. I stood at the back door in my white Army nurse tunic and cunt cap on my head, my pockets loaded with hash. As soldiers passed through the door, I would ask them if they were looking for hash, and almost everyone was. I would sell five grams for $10, one right after the other. I was the last stop on payday, and it paid me good.

I sold more hash than I could have ever smoked, and that's really saying something. Linda smoked a little, but she was never a serious smoker. I smoked enough for the both of us, and that probably didn't help our relationship. The hash was strong, I had ADHD, and every time I smoked it was inevitable that I would get sidetracked, which frustrated the living hell out of her. One time Linda asked me to pick up the mail and stop for some ice and bread before coming home. I was always stoned so I always forgot things she asked me to pick up after my workday. I made it all the way home and realized I had not done the simple task she had asked of me. In an effort to fix my mistake, we jumped in the Volkswagen and ran back to town to get everything she needed. I ran into the store and got to talking and forgot what I had even gone in there to get; I never gave it another thought as I returned to the car empty handed. When I got back Linda asked, "Where's the ice and milk?" The ice and milk were still in the store.

I used to think Linda and I had fallen out of love, but now I don't believe we were ever in love. Perhaps the best times we had in our marriage happened overseas when we finally got to travel Europe. I know it was for me.

Gas was cheap and we got rations to use while we traveled. I was constantly buying and working on used cars to get us from here to there. I was able to work on cars at the base, with access to every kind of tool I might possibly need. So, I would buy a cheap car, drive the hell out of it, and then get another one. We became road warriors! We went to Paris on about $90 in a Volkswagen. We rented a guest house for several days and saw the sights, the subway, the Mona Lisa and other art. The only thing we didn't do was tour the Eiffel Tower. It cost $3 a piece to tour the tower, and we just didn't have the extra cash for that. We traveled cheap. We didn't eat in restaurants; we went to butcher shops and bought sandwich fixings, then we went to the park and drank wine with our sandwiches. We didn't get to do all the fancy shit in France, but we did see a lot and we made a lot of memories. I can still see the Dutch windmills turning.

We went to Amsterdam, but even back then drugs were legal there. You could buy drugs right in front of the cops and no one batted an eye. We walked through the red light district where the prostitutes sat in windows on ornate chairs for window shopping purposes. We visited the Van Gogh Museum, we passed big Dutch windmills in the country and pulled over when we saw signs for cheese. We bought a huge gouda cheese wheel that was about five inches thick for $11. It was delicious and thank god, because we had a lot of it.

We visited Southern Bavaria at Berchtesgaden, south of Munich. We stayed in a cabin in the Bavarian Alps and slept on a feather bed. We visited the castles Neuschwanstein & Linderhofin Füssen & Herrenchiemsee on Chiemsee Lake. We went to Octoberfest in Munich, and we even scored tickets to the 1972 Olympic games. Unfortunately, during the early morning hours of September 5, a Palestinian terrorist group called Black September, stormed the Olympic Village apartment where the Israeli athletes were staying, killing two and taking nine others hostage. The terrorists took the hostages in hopes of exchanging them for 230 Arab prisoners. The Olympics were suspended for 24 hours, so we didn't get to go. I still have my tickets though. We visited a Monastery southeast of Munich, near the edge of the Black Forest on a Sunday afternoon. On Sundays, they served bratwursts and beer in the monastery basement. They would sell you a liter of beer, and it was strong. I drank mine and half of Linda's. We all got tore down drunk and ended up in Munich instead of Augsburg. We just kept going around and around the turnabout in downtown. We finally stopped and everyone just got out to pee right there in public. We couldn't wait anymore. I ended up puking all down the Autobahn.

At one point we ponied up the cash for airfare to Athens, Greece. We rented a little hotel that offered breakfast, which ensured we had at least one meal a day. We took tours and saw the Parthenon. Hell, I even took a marble rock from the Parthenon. We immersed ourselves in the culture, even the parts we didn't like, such as ouzo. Greeks drink ouzo with everything and it is disgusting, but we can say we tried it.

As time passed, I kept wheeling and dealing hash, buying and working on used cars, selling my rations, and burning up the roads. We were finally ready to take our biggest trip yet. I had recently read, The Drifter by James Mitchener; one of the few books I've ever read in my life. It was about hippies drifting through Europe, Spain, and Africa. The book inspired even more wanderlust within me, and I began planning out a trip that would closely resemble the one I had read about. I took eighteen days' worth of leave and we struck out to hit all the cities listed in the book. Linda was seven and a half months pregnant with our daughter, Tracy, but that didn't stop us.

We travelled down to France, then on to Spain where we immersed ourselves in the area culture with a bus ride full of people and livestock. We visited Barcelona then Madrid. While in Madrid we met another American traveler named Mark. He travelled with us for a few days, and before he left our company, he got our address. He came to visit us once back in Germany. We drove through the flat dry lands south of Spain some 300 miles until we reached the ocean, where cliffs were lined with white stucco houses. We took a ferry across the westernmost part of the Mediterranean Sea to Ceuta, located on a small peninsula, before crossing into Africa. We ventured as far south as Rabat, the Capital of Morocco. We saw breathtaking views and bought gulame beads by the pound to bring back to our friends.

Linda began to grow uncomfortable from all the car time. She was unable to lay on her back because sometimes the pressure would make her faint, and she couldn't lay on her stomach for obvious reasons. I found an empty beach and pulled over. I dug a hole in the sand so she could lay comfortably on her belly in the sand and relax. It was the most romantic thing I ever did for Linda. On the way home the car started acting up in France. We didn't think we were going to make it back. We did make it all the way back to the apartment, where the car died for good. It was a miracle the car made it that far.

Our sightseeing days ended just as Tracy was set to arrive. She was born frank breech at the hospital I worked at. I still have the x-ray. Her legs were folded up with her feet at her shoulders and she was sucking her thumb. It was a hard labor for Linda, but she and Tracy pulled through beautifully. I was so fortunate to be there and watch my daughter being born, to catch her, and take her to the nursery. I remember taking her to the nursery, wrapped snugly in a blanket. Once we got to the nursery we unwrapped her, and her little legs were still folded up around her shoulders. When we laid her on her back, her little feet would almost touch her ears. It was so funny and adorable. Little did I know that she would turn out to be the gem of a person that she is today, whom I love so dearly.

Not long after Tracy was born, my time in Germany began to wind down, so I sent my family home to the States and started getting ready to say so long to the Army and my friends. I also needed time to figure out how I was going to take my new business venture home with me. I had learned the trade, or art, of selling hash and I was hooked on the extra cash. I knew I needed to figure out how to get some of that hash back home. I had so many kinds of hash in Germany, but some of the best I had was green. In general, the best hash was supposedly black and came from Pakistan, and laced with opium. Then, red hash was supposed to be the next best and was typically from Lebanon. Brown hash from Morocco was okay, but not great quality, and green hash was supposedly at the bottom of the barrel. Today, you might compare green hash to the pot that comes out of Mexico. You can smoke a thousand bowls and never really get high. Even so, the best hash I ever had my hands on was green. It was called Trip Green, and it was worth every dime. You could smoke a little and take off. It was damn good stuff!

I scored a kilo of red hash and came up with an idea to get it back home. I was always on post working on cars, processing film, and building my own furniture. I decided to put my hands to work building a chessboard, which was really just a container for a kilo of hash. I crafted a very nice chessboard with a secret compartment. I wrapped the hash, which came in a burlap sack with a blue stamp on it and sandwiched it inside the chessboard between some quarter inch particle board and three-quarter inch wood, secured it with nails, sanded and shellacked it, and prepared to send it home to the states as part of my "whole baggage." I was so paranoid about flying the hash back in the chessboard, but it made it without a hitch. Even after arriving home and moving back to Natchitoches, I was still too paranoid to open it. Three months went by, and I decided it was safe to take out the hash, and if it wasn't, then fuck it; I needed the money. I chiseled open the chest, and just like that I was back in business.

Chapter Seven: The High Life

Linda and I found an apartment for $80 a month in downtown Natchitoches, behind McCain Hardware when I came home from Germany. My frat buddy Jim had moved back to town, and it was great to have him around. We stayed with him the first couple of weeks after we moved back to Natchitoches while we fixed up the apartment. Every day we would go over to the apartment and work on it. It was a real dump. We patched and painted, put linoleum down, and got it cleaned up. It looked so great that the renter across the hall was jealous. Oddly enough, a friend of mine from Texas that I'd met during my service in Germany moved to town and rented the apartment downstairs. He met a girl and they shacked up there for a few months then moved on. It was fun having him as a neighbor for a little while. We would go out and pick mushrooms, smoke hash, and trip.

We visited Linda's parents with the new baby and left with her dad's white Chevy pickup. We were living on my G.I. Bill, which was about $425 a month. We stretched that while we both went back to school. Linda worked on her teaching certificate while I worked to become a nurse, so that I could go to anesthesia school. While I was in still Germany, I had spoken to a nurse anesthetist who was married to a captain. I would talk to her a lot, and she convinced me to go to nursing school and anesthesia school. She said because I was a man, I would make a fortune in the industry. Before I ever set foot back on American soil, I had it all planned out. I'd go to Northwestern in Natchitoches for one year, then move to Shreveport.

The first time I went to college I never applied myself; I didn't have to. I could slide by doing next to nothing and still pass. The second time I went to school, I knew exactly what I wanted to do, and I wanted to be good at it. I wanted to study and read to make good grades. My physiology teacher could lecture and write on the board as fast as he spoke. He really challenged me. I copied his notes and listened very intently. His tests were all essays, so I just memorized his notes and aced the class. He tried to convince me to go into physiology and I told him, "No, I want to make money. I can make more as a nurse anesthetist than as a professor." Sad, but totally true.

Coming back to Natchitoches from Germany was a shock to my system. We were broke all over again and I was clinically depressed. I was a grown man, but often found myself crying like a baby on my porch steps. We had led a party life in Germany and traveled Europe. And every moment we weren't traveling we'd spent planning the next trip. Now my life was filled with boring schoolwork, a woman I didn't love, and a baby. That was a long year.

It was only a matter of time before I got sick of being broke. Three months in, I decided to pull out the chessboard and get to work.

I pulled out the kilo of red Lebanese hash that I had flown home from Germany. I started selling hash for $10 a gram to two friends I met at Northwestern. I smoked about an eighth of what I smuggled back and sold the rest to Rick and Rapper.

Rick and Rapper became very good friends of mine, and I kept up with them for many years. Rapper had been the reporter for the college newspaper. After I left Natchitoches for Shreveport, Rapper went to a Jim Croce concert, where he got to get up close and personal with Jim. He took several photos with him before and after the show. That same night, Croce died in a plane accident. I was told that his plane was searched for drugs, or going to be searched, and they were in a hurry to leave. The plane took off but crashed in the woods. A few months later, Rapper showed me the photos of Croce. I told him he should contact his wife and let her know he had the last photos taken of him while he was alive, but I don't know if he ever did.

I was able to support my family with the hash money, and I was able to buy myself a used Honda motorcycle. It was the biggest piece of crap in the world. It had an aluminum block engine and always stripped the screws, but when it was running it ran like a bat out of hell. I always looked for opportunities to sell pot because I liked to smoke it, but I never liked to buy it. It was $10 a bag, and that seemed like a lot at the time. If I sold it, I was able to smoke for free. When the hash ran out at the end of the year, I started selling $10 bags of shitty Mexican weed. If you smoked the whole bag at once you might get a little high, but then again, you might not.

I finished up my sciences at Northwestern and we moved to Shreveport so I could start nursing school, because there were a lot of clinical sites in the area. We rented a great little 1920's two-bedroom house with a detached garage, in the South Shreveport area for about a year. Then we moved closer to my school, into a big two-story house in the South Highland area for about $150 a month. The house was on a hill and had big steps leading up to the porch with a swing, hardwood floors throughout, a library, pocket doors, window seats, and plenty of space to move around. We lived there for about a year. I grew a couple of small marijuana plants inside to keep me smoking while I went to school and worked as an orderly. Our lives together were separate for the most part, but the house made it look and feel like we were doing what we thought we were supposed to be doing. I took a job as an orderly working from 3p.m. to 11 p.m. at the hospital while I was going to school and Linda did her student teaching assignment in Caddo Parish. We bought a boat, and we would go ski on Black Bayou in Benton every chance we had. Man, we loved being at the lake. We would ski all day, have fried chicken picnics, nap in the sun, play with Tracy, and every time, for a few minutes, it seemed like we could make it. There were days when life on Black Bayou didn't seem so bad, but my infidelity said otherwise. I was being unfaithful to Linda and was engaged in multiple affairs. My marriage to Linda ended for me on the Seawall in Galveston that day, yet there I was on Black Bayou with my wife.

Tracy was getting older, my marriage to Linda was totally in the shitter, and my job at the hospital consisted of a lot of enemas and colonoscopy preps. The only positive thing during this time was the birth of my son, Brian. Children are a blessing, but anyone who has raised one knows it's a tough gig on a good day.

Finally, I had a stroke of good luck.

There was a new profession beginning to catch on called respiratory therapy and the hospital saw an opportunity to expand services and bill for their services by hiring a department head. They hired Dave Valeton, a registered respiratory therapist with a Bachelor of Science degree, as the department head. Respiratory therapy was a relatively new practice. Dave was the first brilliant person I had ever met. Over the years I have had the good fortune of meeting and working with some brilliant and gifted people, but Dave was the first. He received his Registered Respiratory Therapist license in New Orleans when it was a written test but also a question-and-answer session which had to be satisfied verbally in front of a three-person panel. The panel usually consisted of an anesthesiologist, pulmonologist, and respiratory therapist. The verbal test had a 50% fail rate, so they eventually created a clinical simulation. Students had to explain how to do things like intubate a patient and calculate vent settings. The system worked much better for everyone.

When Dave saw that I was determined and working to get my nursing BS, he asked me to work with him and told me that he would teach me respiratory therapy. He said he needed people who could think, and he felt like I was that person. I asked what the requirements were, and he told me he needed forty hours per week. We worked out a schedule that allowed me to finish school. It was a great situation to find myself in. I was learning from the best, and I was making extra money because they could call me in to do arterial blood gases on patients and we were paid by the procedure. Everything was finally moving in the right direction to allow me to have some financial success.

A big year was 1976. Brian was born, I graduated from nursing school in Shreveport, and I left Linda. We couldn't get along to save our lives, but somehow managed to make another baby before calling it quits. We agreed to separate and file for divorce, although we didn't file for divorce immediately. I helped Linda move out and found another house for her and the kids. I found a great house in a shitty neighborhood for $18,000 and remodeled it. It wasn't ideal, but it was the best I could do. I have always said I married for the wrong reasons, and I stayed for the wrong reasons, too.

After I moved Linda out, I moved some roommates in. Jesse and Alise were my new roommates and we liked to party. They were still in nursing school, and I was working in respiratory therapy. Alise and I had a great thing going. We would cruise the bars together and if one of us got lucky and picked someone up that was great, but if one of us didn't get lucky, we went home and made our own luck. It was actually pretty perfect. A few months later I thought I fell in love with a married woman on the night shift, and that was fun for a while. I was trying to find myself in the women I dated. It was all the better if I found myself in them physically.

All the while, even after becoming a father for the second time, working in respiratory therapy, and leaving Linda, I was still selling crappy pot. It was $10 a bag and you couldn't smoke enough to get high.

Rapper convinced me that he had a plan and a new connection for some Columbian gold bud in New Orleans. It was $300 per pound, and I didn't think I could sell it at that price and make any money. Who in the hell had that kind of money back then? But Rapper was convinced I could sell it and Ziggy, who lived down the street, assured me that we could get rid of it. Ziggy was the kind of guy who never wanted to put up money for anything. He would say, "We can get rid of it," but that meant I had to front all the money. I thought on it and decided to take the risk. I took the $300 intended for my car note and rent money and went to New Orleans to buy a pound. Rapper was right. By the next day I had sold it all. I took the $600 in my hand and went straight back and bought two pounds, and within three hours it was all sold. At this point, I was selling for $40 a bag and I was back to doubling my money again. I had friends that would buy ten bags at a time, go sell those and come back for more. I went from being broke to having over $10,000 in about two months. That was a lot of money in 1977. I had never held so much money in my hand at one time. It provided, to say the least. I was Columbian gold struck, and business was booming!

I would run to New Orleans and buy pounds from Rapper. While I was there, we'd go to jazz concerts and party. I'd bring the pounds back to Shreveport, where I had expanded my marijuana operation. I would give my friends ten bags each and tell them they owed me $400. I told them I didn't care if they sold them, stepped on them, or rolled joints with them, but I

91

wanted my $400. And like clockwork, in a matter of mere days, every single one of them would come back with the money they owed me and get more pot to sell. My side business kept me running back and forth to New Orleans constantly. In fact, I was making so much money that I was starting to think I didn't really need to go to anesthesia school!

Almost as soon as I thought about ditching out on anesthesia school, I got an acceptance letter from the school in Wichita Falls, Texas. I was excited but I was making a shit ton of money. I had more than $25,000 in a matter of no time, and I really liked having that kind of money. The money made an easy decision a lot harder than it should have been. In the end, I told myself I needed to follow my dream. I kept my head down and kept dealing as much pot as possible before it was time to go to Wichita Falls.

At one point, I got so sick of driving to New Orleans that I decided to just fly down there, make the deal, and fly back. I was so busy selling drugs that I just didn't have the time to waste. I was moving about twenty to thirty pounds every two months and getting ready to go to school. I decided I didn't have time to waste on the road trip, so I bought a roundtrip ticket to New Orleans from Shreveport. I brought a huge, old, brown hard-shell suitcase to bring back my haul. As soon as I landed, I rented a car and drove to Rapper's house. There, I packed seventeen pounds of marijuana down into trash bags, then I packed the trash bags down into that old, brown suitcase. I forced the lid closed with my weight and locked the latches. When I got to the airport, I tossed the suitcase on the baggage belt and watched it disappear. I couldn't carry that big thing on, so away it went. When I landed in Shreveport, I rushed to the baggage claim area to look for my cargo. When that old, brown suitcase came out, so did the undeniable smell of marijuana. I picked it up, walked calmly to my car in the parking lot, and drove home. It's a miracle I didn't get caught, but it only made me feel more invincible. In reality, that trip should have been a red flag that I was getting careless.

Ziggy called me up one day and asked me to come over and hang out. He lived just a few houses down from me. I walked down to hang out for a while, while he worked on his chopper in the front yard. That was the day he introduced me to a lovely lady— Cocaine.

They call it a lovely lady because it's an intense, romantic love affair from which your thirst cannot be quenched. If cocaine were a woman, she'd be the best sex you ever had. You'd lock yourself in a room with her and use her until she was all gone, or you had faded away. Cocaine was my first true love. My heart raced and fluttered, I felt alive, and I knew I wanted to do it again, and again, and again. It felt like the beginning of a beautiful relationship that filled every void in my life. Ziggy had introduced me to the love of my life. Almost immediately, Ziggy revealed to me that my high could be even better if I shot up. I wasn't even a little scared to try it, and I fell in love all over again.

The thing about cocaine is, one shot is too many and a thousand ain't enough. I was hooked on the first try. Every time

I used, I used everything I had. If I bought a quarter of coke, I would shoot every bit of it up my arm until it was completely gone. I could not stop. My arms quickly began to look like hamburger meat, and I was constantly stopping whatever I was doing to shoot up. Being in the medical field, I knew there was a better way to get my high than constantly poking myself with needles. I brought home an IV pole hooked to a catheter with a stop cock, and viola— Just like that I was an IV cocaine user. I would walk around the house hooked up to the IV all day. Hell, I even answered the door with the IV in my arm on occasion.

I wasn't quite ready to relinquish my lifestyle, or the cash it provided, so I decided to change my strategy. I took on a business partner before I left for anesthesia school. I cut Chuck in on my business, and I started dealing in pounds. He was a great guy, but he was messed up in a lot of ways, which was fine by me because so was I. He was a Vietnam fighter pilot who had flown over fifty missions and had bombed Hanoi. He shared stories with me that were terrible and terrifying. I liked him and he was trustworthy. We became great friends, and we did a lot together— a lot of drugs together. He was my go-between for New Orleans. The plan was for him to make runs to New Orleans when I needed to pick up pot to sell, then meet me in Texas with the drugs while I was in anesthesia school.

One weekend, Chuck and I were supposed to go to New Orleans and pick up thirty pounds of marijuana from Rapper, but we had just gotten a new stash of coke. We had planned to leave by 8 a.m. that morning and had even gotten up a little early to get ready before heading out. We decided to do a little coke before we left. Our intended departure time of 8 a.m. turned into 8 p.m. because we got preoccupied doing coke for over twelve hours. Rapper kept calling and asking where we were, and we kept making excuses. We finally ran out of coke around 8 p.m. and decided we needed to get down to New Orleans to pick up the pot. We were a little afraid that we were going to crash after doing coke all day, so we took some quaaludes. I loved quaaludes. I always thought it was a great high because you're going fast, but you're going smooth. We got about halfway between Baton Rouge and New Orleans, and everything wore off. We were spent, so we pulled over to sleep. Next thing I knew, a state policeman was tapping on the window. I rolled the window down knowing I had $25,000 in my sock to pay for half of my marijuana load. He asked what we were doing, and I told him we had gotten sleepy while driving, so we pulled over to be safe. My heart pounded for a second, but then he said, "You need to pull over in a rest area to sleep," to which I replied, "Oh, yes sir, officer. Will do." We were wide awake after that and drove on into New Orleans to meet Rapper.

Rapper's connection in New Orleans had an incredible smalltime operation based out of Florida. The masterminds of the operation were a group of guys who had smoked pot together in high school. A few of them had stayed in Florida after graduation, while one moved to Chicago, one to Philly, and another to New Orleans. I met some of them in New Orleans at a jazz festival. They had rented a space inside the racetrack and had a Winnebago set up. They had coke and beer, so we partied with them. The ones who stayed in Florida started bringing in marijuana from international waters via boat to a drop off location, about 10 miles off the coast. They worked on commission moving as much marijuana as their boat could carry, then they could either take cash or 10% of the load they were transporting. They stockpiled their marijuana hauls and called their buddies in Chicago, Philly, and New Orleans, who would eventually show up in Florida to retrieve their portion. Rapper and I flew down to Miami once to pick up a load when product had gotten slow, and the transaction process was like none other I had experienced. We went to a plain looking little subdivision called Hollywood. It was probably a ten-block radius, full of little stucco houses. That day was a procession from one garage to the next smoking and trying out pot, like a buffet line. I had never seen so much marijuana! In some places it was literally stacked to the ceiling. Rapper and I had really hit the motherload with this connection. We bought a bale of marijuana for $17,000 and loaded into the rental car. We were unable to cross state lines in the rental car and had to turn it in near the Panama City airport. We pulled in the parking lot around 11:30 p.m. next to our new rental, swapped the bale from one trunk to the other, and took off again! It was such a simpler time back then, and even though there weren't cameras, it was still a bold move.

While my personal life was being shattered by my newfound love for cocaine, my work life was only getting better. I was working at Schumpert Medical in Shreveport when I met a respiratory therapist from California named John Hydell, who was hired to manage the department. He was looking for someone to manage the nightshift and offered me extra pay as a respiratory therapist. I took it.

Ziggy introduced me to his cocaine connection; a guy named Tom Roy. He was supposedly the manager for Supertramp. He lived in a shitty garage apartment and had gold records for Supertramp on the walls. Supposedly the group fired him, but while he was with them, he got to know a lot of people with a lot of coke. We hung out and discussed some business plans while we did coke. I wanted to do more cocaine than I could afford, so I made a deal with Tom and suddenly I was a full-blown cocaine dealer. I got six ounces, at $2,000 a piece. Dealing cocaine was never about the money for me. In fact, I never really made any money off cocaine. I just wanted to sell enough to pay for my habit. What I was getting was about 70% pure, so I could step on it real hard and get rocks for myself. I probably kept about an eighth out of every ounce because I loved coke so much. We did a solid rock that day as we negotiated the details of the deal. The next day I was the most dehydrated I had ever been in my life. Every time I pulled back on the syringe and saw my thick, black blood I would say to myself, "What the fuck are you doing to yourself?" But I kept doing it. The only time you ever start talking to yourself or telling yourself you never need to do coke again is when you just did your last hit and you're totally out.

When the spring rolled around and it was time to head off to anesthesia school in Wichita Falls, I was all set. Because I had made the business decision to take on a great partner like Chuck, I would still be able to have plenty of pot to smoke, plenty of coke to shoot, and keep making money hand over fist while I went to school. It was a classic scenario for having my cake and eating it, too. I was living the dream and could not see it was turning into a nightmare.

I moved to Wichita Falls in the spring for anesthesia school where I fit right in. There was an incredible amount of drug use at school and in the circle I ran in. This made it easy to find people to sell drugs to. For the most part, if you weren't totally fucked up or drunk, no one seemed to care. Anesthesia school was different from most graduate programs. It was loosely put together for experience and to gain credentials, but mostly to make money for the hospitals. I thought there would be lectures and clinicals, but it was more or less a sweat farm. I had one scheduled class my first semester that usually lasted all of about ten minutes, and then we were to report to emergency room floor for work. As freshmen we worked 24 hours on and 24 hours off, and we were responsible for the emergency room. The upperclassmen would wonder in and administer anesthetic, when necessary, then go back to bed. It was a crazy fastmoving pace.

For six months I partied hardy in Wichita Falls. I had plenty of money, I was dating the best-looking girl in the O.R., the doctors were pissed, and everyone was jealous. It was epic! I was still dealing drugs and I was burning up the road between Wichita Falls and Shreveport.

Nothing could stop me, not even an ice storm. One time, just before the end of the first semester, I made a run back to Shreveport to pick up thirty pounds. On the way back to Wichita Falls, I was flying along and started noticing cars and trucks in the ditches. The more cars I saw in the ditch the more I thought those idiots just didn't know how to drive in a little bad weather. Then I ended up in a full spin and hit the ditch. I slammed into the ditch sideways, and both of my tubeless tires collapsed. It was freezing, but I couldn't just sit there, I had shit to do! I jacked up my car, took off the tires, put my spare on one, and then hitched a ride to the tire shop in town to have the other repaired. I left thirty pounds of marijuana in the trunk of my car, sitting in the ditch on the side of the road, while I had my tires reinflated. When I got back to the car, everything was just as I left it, so I put my tire on and went on about my business.

I was a lucky sonofabitch on more than one occasion, but perhaps the luckiest I ever got was one day when I was on the side of the road near Terrell, Texas shooting up. I had been pulling over every few minutes to shoot up on the way to Shreveport. I pulled over near a shady little no star motel in my black Mercury Monarch. I had an ounce of coke open in the seat. I put a towel under my arm and pulled the rubber cord tight. I pulled the rock, broke it down, and stuck the needle in my arm. About the time I was getting ready to push, I looked up and a policeman had pulled up next to my driver's side window and rolled his window down. I was on a slight incline which kept him from being able to see inside of my car. I rolled my window down with the needle still in my arm and the officer asked what I was doing. I told him I had gotten sleepy and pulled over to be safe. Satisfied, he told me I could stay there until nightfall and went on. If he had caught me, I would have pushed that cocaine, thinking it could be my last hit. But it wasn't my last hit, so I pushed it in celebration and away I went to Shreveport.

I was out of control and had been for a while. The most important thing in the world to me was drugs, and to make matters worse, I couldn't keep my mouth shut. There were points when I looked into the mirror and asked myself, "What the fuck are you doing? You're an educated person." Everyone knew I was in too deep. Not only was I dealing marijuana and cocaine, but I now had easy access to almost anything you could want at the hospital, and there was almost nothing I wouldn't try. For instance, I tried Ketamine once. Ketamine was a drug used for conscious sedation. I had given it to patients before and watched their eyes go dark as they drifted off somewhere. I wanted to know where they went and how it felt, so I injected it into myself. I collapsed on the bathroom floor for several minutes. I really thought I was immortal by that point.

I was living the high life until I let my alligator mouth overload my hummingbird ass. Eventually, I had partied so much and run my mouth so much, that the school asked me to resign. I dug my heels in just enough and negotiated. I asked them if they were asking me to resign from school based on my performance, and insisted they give me a letter of recommendation for another anesthesia school. I told them I would quietly resign if they gave me a letter. They obliged just to get me the hell out of there. In six short months I had risen high and fast, and fallen faster and harder. I moved back to Shreveport with dashed dreams but little care. But this wasn't rock bottom; not even close.

Chapter Eight: A Big Deal

I packed up my apartment in Wichita Falls and headed back to Shreveport after being asked to resign from anesthesia school. I moved into a nice little house by myself and got my old job back at the hospital. I was living so carelessly. Someone broke into my house and stole about a quarter of an ounce of coke from me before I even unpacked my moving boxes. I will always wonder if I knew the person who broke in and stole that coke from me, but I was honestly just thankful that whoever it was didn't look in the closet because there were twenty pounds of gold bud Columbian in there. So, I moved in with Chuck, my friend and business partner, on Finley Drive. It made more sense to have someone at the house all the time to keep an eye on the drugs and someone to split the bills with. I took my unpacked boxes to the new place, but I didn't bother unpacking them there 0either, because I thought I had better shit to do.

I was bummed out about anesthesia school, using coke constantly, and missing a lot of work. I kept all my clients in Wichita Falls and continued to make deliveries to Texas regularly. Not long after I got kicked out of school, a huge tornado came through and flattened Wichita Falls. People died, there were hundreds of injuries, and the town was devastated. When I went back to make a delivery I drove by my old apartment, and there was nothing left but the swimming pool. I started thinking about how lucky I was, and that if I hadn't gotten kicked out of school I might have died in that tornado. It almost felt like fate had intervened, and my sense of purpose was briefly renewed as I thought I had been spared for better things.

But unless better things consisted of partying night and day, that was not the case. I was smoking pot all day and partying somewhere every night. We went to gay bars and disco clubs. We carried little vials of coke on a chain, with a little spoon in our pocket. Every night we had something going on. I was small fries compared to a lot of guys, but everyone knew I had the drugs they wanted, even the people who couldn't pay for them. I had access to so much marijuana that I never smoked a joint all the way down. I always had about half of an inch left over, so anyone who saw the ashtray in my car was inclined to ask for my roaches. Hell, my roaches were practically a joint. But I always had plenty to share and felt generous giving them my leftover joints. I was more than happy to give them those roaches because I was just grateful not to be the person asking for someone's leftover joint.

We were also doing a lot of mushrooms when I came back to Shreveport. Spring was in the air and mushrooms were on the cow shit. They were free and I loved to trip. We would slip out to a cow pasture and pull the mushrooms off the dried cow patties and take them home. Some people liked to make mushroom tea, but it literally tasted like cow shit. I would have just rather eaten the shitty mushrooms than drink that shitty tea. While I was in college, I figured out a way to make taking mushrooms a little easier. I would take a whole mushroom and chop it up in the blender, add one ounce of Hawaiian punch concentrate, blend it together and put it in a shot glass. One gulp and you had it.

My life was spiraling in Shreveport. I was living a scumbag life and it was catching up to me. When I did go into work, I was running to the bathroom every 15 minutes to do a jack of coke. I was losing my grip on reality every day and going further and further down a road that I couldn't turn back on.

Ziggy was in over his head in every way by this point, and not only was he ruining his life, but he was also ruining mine. He was completely strung out and he had not been selling the coke he was getting from me. Every bit was going straight up his arm. He racked up about $7,000 in coke that he owed me. He had to sell in order to pay me back, but I could no longer front him the coke, which meant I had to go to every single transaction with him. Things were not going well, and he was constantly making it worse.

Ziggy continued to beg me for coke, saying he wanted to pay me back. He didn't give a shit about paying me back. Ziggy only cared about himself, like every other drug addict out there. He kept his ex-meth head girlfriend around for sex and drug connections. She was riddled with pimples and boils from the bad meth she was shooting. She was a big problem, along with her meth head father and brother who were burglars. They had recently gone to jail in Caddo Parish for theft and needed her help to get out. They were lowlife thieves and meth addicts, but the cops were interested in bigger fish. Law enforcement approached Ziggy's ex-girlfriend about helping them with another case they had been working, and in turn they would drop the charges against her father and brother. They wanted Ziggy and his cocaine source—me.

I don't know if Ziggy knew what was going on, or if he was just so strung out that he didn't care about anything but his next hit. I would like to believe, and usually choose to believe, that he had no idea that his ex-girlfriend was setting me up. She introduced him to two undercover agents posing as cowboys with pockets full of cash and looking to score big deals. He started riding me about buying and selling in bigger volumes. He was relentless. He pushed hard, and harder under the guise of friendship, supposedly because he so badly wanted to pay me back the money he owed. I resisted a little longer.

About the time that Ziggy began to harass me about doing bigger deals, I received a warning from a friend. One night while I was walking around the house hooked up to my coke IV pole, per usual, a buddy of mine came to the house. He told me he believed the house was being watched. He said that for the last few days there had been two guys staked out at the end of the street, and that they followed anyone seen coming and going from my house. I didn't really listen to this warning. Whether I felt invincible, or whether I was just an addict who couldn't do any better, I just didn't listen. And I sure as hell didn't change my behavior for the better. Instead, I made worse decisions than ever before for the next few weeks. I had become a total junkie and was completely reckless. I was rarely going in to work, but when I did, I spent a fair amount of time in the bathroom shooting up just to get through the day. On one such occasion, I realized I did not have a clean needle when I went into the bathroom. I had just come from administering a breathing treatment and remembered I had the tuberculin syringe from my last patient. One of the drugs used in breathing treatments is Isuprel. It's a lot like a shot of adrenaline. I needed to get high and that's what I had on hand, so I drew up the coke shot in the used syringe and pushed. My heart rate skyrocketed, but I knew what was causing it to race, so I just waited there in the bathroom for it to wear off. After a few minutes I went back to work, for about fifteen or twenty minutes... until I needed another hit. My life was spiraling out of control, and I didn't even notice.

Ziggy kept pushing for me to sell bigger quantities of coke to two interested buyers he had lined up. I kept telling him I didn't want to meet any new people, and I didn't want or like to move so much product at one time. At first, he wanted me to sell an ounce of coke to the guys. He kept telling me, "C'mon, man, it's an ounce of coke! That's $2,000!" Ziggy was right. It was a lot of money to turn your nose up at. And knowing that, he wore me down and I finally caved into his request.

The first deal went down in a shady motel parking lot off North Market. They pulled up in a Volkswagen and wanted more coke than I had on me. I sold them an ounce, even though I knew it felt all wrong. I was not accustomed to doing business like that. Normally, I did business in my living room with people I knew and had vetted. I told Ziggy not to ever ask to bring those motherfuckers around me again. Something was off and I didn't trust those guys, but Ziggy kept pushing.

"C'mon, man! They want six ounces! SIX OUNCES," he would say, backing me into a corner. And six ounces of cocaine was a lot of damn money, and it was also a lot of damn coke for me. I went to my coke connection and bought six ounces. I told Ziggy I would only sell them three ounces, and if everything went well, I'd sell them three more in a day or so.

The next deal went down in a second story hotel room, at the Riverboat Inn on Monkhouse Drive off Interstate 20. I never carried a gun until I started dealing drugs. Hell, I didn't even carry one in the Army, but just a few months earlier I had purchased a beautiful 9 mm Belgium-made Browning automatic. Purchasing that pistol should have been a sign that I was in over my head. Before I left the house that day, I shoved the 9 mm in the back of my pants and drove to the hotel. Absolutely nothing felt right about the situation. In fact, it all felt wrong, but I pushed the hesitancy aside.

Ziggy and his girlfriend pulled up, then he and I went upstairs to the room while she waited in the car. When we approached the room, I immediately noticed the curtains were open and the window was about half open. The first thing I did when we walked in was shut the curtains. The cowboys had asked for six ounces of cocaine, but I intentionally only brought three ounces. I held one back and planned to present them with two ounces. They pulled out the cash, I pulled out the coke, then they pulled out their badges. The third ounce was discovered during the arrest and search of my vehicle.

For a brief moment, my fight or flight senses took over. I was busted and didn't want to go to prison. I reached around my back for the 9 mm, but they immediately drew their firearms and said, "Don't do it." I had my wits about me enough not to start a shootout or resist arrest. I was lucky and I had been smart enough to close the curtains when I arrived. Had the sniper who was positioned outside seen me reach for my gun, my story would have ended that day at the River Boat Inn.

Two great American heroes died that day— one in spirit and another in the flesh. John Wayne died the same day I was arrested. The headlines of his passing in the newspaper where my crime was reported overshadowed my arrest but ingrained the date of his death in my mind. I wasn't a hero, and he really wasn't either, but it made people laugh when I said it.

The truth is, they could have arrested me on the first deal, but they didn't know if we were armed, and they didn't have backup. Plus, they knew I'd be back to sell them more. They had already figured out that I couldn't say no to that kind of money, and that I couldn't say no to Ziggy. On the second deal, they were ready.

They handcuffed me at the Riverboat Inn, and I sat there for about an hour while they collected evidence and congratulated each other. My mind raced as I tried to flesh out a plan that extended far beyond the inevitable prison time I was facing. They couldn't keep me forever, and hopefully not even very long since I had never been in trouble before. Unless you count the time I was arrested and fined in college for having some panties thrown over my shoulder after a panty raid, but that got dismissed. As soon as the handcuffs went on, I began to brainstorm how and when I would be able to get my nursing license back and how I would get back into anesthesia school. In fact, one of the very first things I did after the arrest was arrange for my anesthesia books to be sent to me immediately. I suddenly desperately wanted to protect my career that I had been pissing away for the last few years. It was in that moment, at the Riverboat Inn, that I decided no matter what it took and no matter what it cost— I would get my life back. Next time, I wouldn't fuck it up.

They took me downtown, where I sat around for another hour before they started booking me in, then they threw me in a holding cell at Caddo Parish Prison, about twenty minutes northwest of Shreveport in Keithville. I was shuffled in with other prisoners and we were separated into two categories— convicted and unconvicted, or sentenced and unsentenced. I spent the next twenty-five days in maximum security, inside a 4x6 cell, until I was taken out for arraignment. My bond was set at $100,000, on the premise that I would go into the Odyssey House drug rehab treatment program in New Orleans. I had $25,000 worth of marijuana and coke in my safe that I intended to use to pay for my attorney. Unfortunately, my girlfriend at the time, flushed all the coke and pot I had, that I'd planned to use to make bail. Neither the house nor the lease were in my name and would never have been searched, but she panicked. My parents tried to get some family members to give them money for my bail, but they couldn't pull the money together. They had to put their house up against the bond for me to get out of jail and enter the program. I felt terrible about that, but I felt terrible about everything at that point because I was so strung out, and my entire life and career had been shattered in a matter of minutes in a single night.

Chapter Nine: Odyssey

I hired Jack Wellbourne Jr., a prominent criminal attorney in Shreveport. The intent was to get me into a rehab as soon as possible and use that as a mechanism to get probation, and it worked. I had no prior felonies, I had a degree, I had a profession, and I had children. There was hope! I spent the next three months learning the ropes at Odyssey House before my sentencing date. After I made bond, I shuffled from the court room in shackles back to the holding cell. I was released on bond at that time and put on a van headed to Odyssey House in the Big Easy. There was nothing easy about that shit.

An odyssey is a long wandering or voyage marked by many changes of fortune while searching for something. It's an intellectual or spiritual awakening that comes to passthrough hardships. It's a quest, often plagued by peril. The word odyssey was made famous by Homer's Odyssey, the Greek poem, and epic story about a ten-year struggle to return home after the Trojan war. The work is filled with mythical creatures, wrath of gods, vengeance, perseverance, perception of reality versus reality, and spiritual growth. Homer refers to his protagonist as "wily Odysseus," but not because of his bravery or strength. Rather, because he was incredibly clever. Perhaps, if I had been more clever, I wouldn't have ended up in a van headed for Odyssey House drug rehabilitation program in New Orleans.

Odyssey House was a strange place and my time there was extremely odd. From being in rehab with one of the Neville brothers, to all of the weird rules, my time at Odyssey was a bizarre series of shit shows, and my life wasn't any better because of it. Upon arrival, you become a candidate N who is seeking acceptance as a level one. The house staff removed everything from you, right down to your underwear and socks, then they handed you some clothes that probably came from Goodwill and made you look like a hobo. Once dressed in your new duds, you started meeting with staff to tell them your story, what kind of drugs you did and any problems you might have. You had to convince them that you wanted to be there and that you wanted the treatment. Once you divulged all your shortcomings and begged to be part of and accepted into the program, they used the information gathered at your weakest and most vulnerable state to use as humiliation tools. I had wept when I told my story. My emotions were incredibly raw. I hadn't done any drugs in almost a month, and my entire life seemed to be over. Because I cried, I had to wear a sign for the first two weeks that said, "If you see me feeling sorry for myself, kick me until I stop crying." It was like rubbing salt in a wound every time you passed your peers, who were also house residents.

There were lots of rules, some of which were flatly stupid, and the human dynamics created by drug addicts made it an interesting experience you wished you were not having. Odyssey House was basically a place to teach drug addicts how to do all of the things they already knew how to do but didn't, with a military fashion flair. It was about teaching people how to be responsible for their own lives and how to show up and do a job, while simulating something like military basic training. It was over the top and so elementary to me, but it was better than going to prison.

There were four levels that needed to be mastered before completing the Odyssey House program. Upon arrival, you become a Level One. Level ones are responsible for nothing and never left alone, with the exception of going to the bathroom or taking a shower. That meant you spent a lot of time doing shitty jobs around the house like mopping or dusting while they walked around performing white glove inspections of your work. If you made it to Level Two, and not everyone did, you then became responsible for things such as getting stuff together like mops and brooms. Level Ones and Twos had to be extra careful not to put themselves in a compromising position to screw up in any way. The consequences were steep. For instance, if a Level One or Two was cleaning the porch and jumped, or even tripped, off the porch, they were out of the program because they knew they were not supposed to leave the house, and that included getting off the porch in any way. Depending on the severity of the offense, they might have the option to start all over, which sucked, but went much faster the second time and was still much better than going to prison. Level Threes became responsible for other people. If a Level Three and another person left the house, the Level Three was responsible for making sure both people got back to the house on time. If you made it to Level Four life got a lot better, or at least it did for me. Level Fours became responsible for themselves again. We were responsible for going to work every day and doing the things necessary to survive. Level Fours, the cream of the Odyssey crop, were responsible for big jobs on projects conjured up by New Orleans big wigs and social elites who liked to splash money around for causes and business ventures.

When you became a member of the Odyssey community you had to follow the house's cardinal rules. Anyone who broke the rules had to start the program over or go to prison. The five rules were:

1. No drugs or alcohol
2. No sex
3. No violence or threats of violence
4. No Stealing
5. No knowledge of.

They had you coming and going and if you got in trouble, they worked your ass off. If you screwed up and broke a house rule, you had to start over from the beginning. And "No knowledge of" was a broad and unfair rule that only tainted the humanity of the whole experience even further. For instance, say your best buddy in the program was a Level Two and he admits to you, a Level Four, that he smoked a joint last night— You didn't participate in it, but you knew about it. If he got busted and they found out that you knew he had broken the rules and didn't turn him in, then you went down too; and the whole house went on lockdown. Anyone who fessed up had to start the whole program over.

One time, right after I had just made it to Level Three, this crazy chick went to group therapy and had a total meltdown. She was sobbing uncontrollably, and everyone was asking her why she was crying. Between the tears she blurted out, "Because I had sex with one of the residents!" You would have thought she confessed to murdering one of the residents. The whole place went on lock down and everyone had to go to their room and close their doors. The staff started drilling her about the incident, and of course she spilled the beans on one or two little things, which led to a choir of canaries. After they were finished interrogating her, they brought in the guy she confessed to having sex with. He was facing ten years in prison. They sat him down in front of the entire Odyssey House support staff. Before his interrogation began, they issued him a warning by telling him they already know what he had done. They told him they were not going to ask because he needed to confess to every house rule that he had broken. They reminded him how important it was not leave out any detail, or any indiscretion, because if he did, they would know, and he would be kicked out of the program and sent back to prison. Well, he sure as hell didn't want to go back to prison so he was more than willing to tell them everything, and I mean everything. He told them shit they had no idea was going on in the house! He not only told them about the sex, but he went on to disclose details about marijuana use, and people's names started popping up left and right as participants, or for having knowledge of. The list was long, but they started calling them in one by one, for the same type of interrogation, and every single one of them sang. There were about sixty residents at the house. By the time it was over, and the lockdown was lifted, there were only eleven of us who hadn't been busted. I didn't have knowledge of anything on that occasion, but one time I did. I knew my buddy Brian had been smoking pot, but he didn't give me up for knowing. I still appreciate that.

Group therapy was a pain in the ass. I understood therapy and I even understood group therapy, but it was still a pain in the ass. Many times, it was just a bunch of bullshit. There were two options in group— You could be the center of attention, or you could sit back and listen and not do the work to move forward. If you talked and participated during group, they rode your ass about everything you said and talked about what a fuck up you were. And if you didn't participate in group, or if you had been an asshole, they punished you with dirty dishes and kitchen duty. What they didn't know was that I loved the kitchen! I got in trouble as much as I could so I could be sent to the kitchen. I could just go to the pots and pans and be by myself. I could do the best job I wanted or the worst job I wanted. The worst part about that was having a bunch of kids who weren't even thirty years old yet tell me what to do. It's not like I never got anything out of group, because I did, even if it was just having the space to vent. I got pissed off just like everyone else from time to time. I was and am only human after all.

It wasn't all bad at Odyssey House. On occasion, we would procure a movie theatre and take the whole house, on a Tuesday night, to the show. One time, I was able to procure a night of dinner theatre in Metairie for everyone. It was a play with Pat Paulson, called Holy Moses or something like that.

They served us dinner and after dinner there was a show. It was great.

We also spent a lot of time working on Odyssey House facilities. While I was there, it seemed like we were always working on the house. They were always in the pits financially, or so they said. We were responsible for making phone calls all day to local merchants around town to ask for donations for the program. I'd call up a paint store and score fifty gallons of paint that had been mixed wrong or had been opened and wasn't quite full. They just wanted it hauled off from their place of business, so we would take it off their hands and paint things around the house.

After about three months at Odyssey House, it was finally time for my sentencing hearing. The "Dis-Honorable" Judge Ballard, as I like to call him, gave me twenty years of hard labor with five years suspended probation, on two conditions. First, I had to complete the Odyssey House drug rehab program, and secondly, I must spend a year in a parish prison to avoid the maximum sentence of twenty years. Twenty years for my first offense, like I was Al Capone or some shit! My attorney told me that because I had received probation, he could have my sentence amended if he ever had to revocate me, so we took the deal.

I was asked to sign a release for my pistol to become property of the police department. If I had not signed it, the pistol would have been destroyed. That seemed like a waste, so I signed it over. But the pistol prompted a conversation between the judge and the Assistant District Attorney that still pisses me off to this day. As I was signing the waiver and getting shackled up, Judge Ballard told the Assistant D.A. that it was highly irregularly that no one had discussed the pistol with him before deciding to give it to the police department. He said, "I might have wanted that pistol." The arrogant sonofabitch that just gave me twenty years on a first offense wanted to keep my pistol for his own personal use or private collection. Call it what you want, but I call that stealing. It reminded me of how a serial killer always takes a trophy from his kill. While they were discussing who would end up with my gun, it occurred to me that judges have entirely too much power. The courtroom is ultimately their kingdom, where they are free to rule with an iron fist or render punishment at any time. Their own behavior goes unchecked, and the wheels of justice don't even turn at all, not even slowly, if their behavior were to ever be called into question.

I went straight from the courtroom in shackles, to the Caddo Parish Prison by bus. Once on the farm, they led us inside and after we were behind bars, they removed our shackles. Then we moved on to classification, again separated into two lines— sentenced and unsentenced, and they determined if you needed to be in maximum security and took your prints. On the way in, I met Lieutenant Manor, and he noticed that I had some education. We spoke briefly and when he realized I could type he asked me if I wanted to go to work for him in about a week. About a week later, I started working in classification. I typed up the fingerprinting cards, and fingerprinted new prisoners as they arrived. Prisoners drifted in two to three times a day, so I stayed busy.

The parish prison housed men and women. I especially liked it when women came through for fingerprinting. One female prisoner especially caught my eye as soon as she walked in the door. Her name was Melanie, and she was a cute little Pat Benatar looking girl. We hit it off immediately and I couldn't get her out of my head.

Shortly after I got the fingerprinting gig, someone decided it was a security issue for me to work in classification and I was moved to the law library. While I was working in the law library, I received a court order regarding my Mercury Monarch that had been confiscated when I was arrested. They wanted to transfer the title out of my name so they could sell the car. I immediately wrote them a letter stating that since I was imprisoned and did not have the financial ability to hire an attorney, they would have to pay my attorney fees so that I could go to court. In the end, the car wasn't worth it to them, so I eventually got it back while I was serving my time at Odyssey House. The only reason I won that battle was because I was in no position to fight it.

I often thought of and occasionally saw the girl who reminded me so much of Pat Benatar, but I knew how to spot an opportunity and take it when it presented itself. Especially if it involved a woman.

G.E.D. classes were offered for women on certain days and men on the other days. The library was the epicenter of the classes, attached to the rec room. There was a very strict system in place to try to deter male and female prisoners from hooking up. They had stringent routines and protocol they followed every time the women entered the library. Everything was locked down in the room and all the bathrooms were searched. There was one girl who used to come by the desk at the library and chat with us. Her name was Angie. She was from Shreveport, and she was cute as hell. I had gotten to know her a little bit. She was going to be there for a while on a drug charge, so I asked her if she wanted to have sex. She said yes!

I was stoked and had it all planned out! I convinced my co-librarian, Joe, to help me pull off a prison hookup. There was only one bathroom in our hall. After inspection, I had Joe lock me and a blanket in the broom closet inside the bathroom. When the girls came for their G.E.D. class that day, he gave Angie the key. She unlocked the closet, I unrolled the blanket, and we had hot and heavy sex on the floor for a few minutes. We didn't have much time, maybe five to seven minutes at the most, but we were considerate. She kept trying to get me off, and I kept saying "No, you go first," because I wanted her to get off, too. And almost as soon as it started, it was over. I unlocked the closet then she walked out first and went back to class. A few minutes later I walked out and went back to the library desk. No one suspected a thing! If we had gotten caught, I would have gotten more time for screwing in the broom closet.

You have to seize the day and take every opportunity. Being in that broom closet waiting for Angie reminded me of the time ol' Boudreaux finally learned to seize the day.

One day, Pierre was paddling down the bayou to Boudreaux's house. When he got there Boudreaux was sitting in a rocker on the front porch of his Creole cottage, rocking back and forth.

Pierre paddled up and said, "Hey, Boudreaux! You wanna come wit me today?"

Boudreaux asked what he was going to do, and Pierre told him he was headed out to catch some nutria. Boudreaux leaned forward in his rocking chair and looked in the pirogue and back at Pierre. "I don't see no trap and I don't see no gun. Just how you gonna get a nutria?" he asked.

Pierre replied, "Oh, I got dis here bucket of Nutra Sweet!"

Boudreaux shook his head and said, "Nah, you go ahead."

That afternoon Pierre paddled back by Boudreaux's house, and his pirogue was loaded down with nutria. Pierre called out to Boudreaux, "Hey, Boudreaux! I sure had me a good day. I'm gonna come by in the mornin' and see if you wanna do somethin'."

Boudreaux scratched his head in bewilderment as Pierre paddled by.

The next morning, Pierre came paddling back down the bayou. Pierre paddled up and said, "Hey, Boudreaux! You wanna come wit me today?"

Boudreaux asked him what he was going to do, and he told him he was headed out to kill some ducks. Boudreaux looked down in the pirogue and said, "I don't see no decoys and I don't see no shotgun. How you gonna get them ducks?"

Pierre held up his hand and said, "I've got dis here roll of duct tape."

Boudreaux shook his head again and said, "Nah, you go ahead."

That afternoon, Pierre came paddling back by with a pirogue full of ducks. Boudreaux was scratching his head in disbelief as Pierre paddled by. "Hey, Boudreaux, I sure had me a good time today. I'll come by in the morning and see if you wanna do something."

The next morning, like clockwork, Pierre came paddling back down the bayou. "Hey, Boudreaux! You wanna come wit me today?" asked Pierre.

Boudreaux asked him, "Whatchu got down there in dat pirogue?"

"Pussywillow," Pierre said.

Boudreaux said, "Let me get my hat."

Ol' Boudreaux finally found something worth seizing the day for, and so did I that day in the broom closet.

Angie was cute, but the female prisoner I had fingerprinted, Melanie, really intrigued me. On certain nights of the week, the male and female prisoners were allowed to attend church together. So, essentially church night was date night. That meant male inmates spent all day trying to iron their pants, shirts, and bandanas. Melanie and I got to know each other on church night. She was serving six months for credit card fraud and hot checks. She treated herself to a trip to New York with the Moody Blues and partied with the Cars and Meatloaf on her aunt's credit card. She was a wild child, but her parents knew the judge and managed to get a deal worked out where she could spend six months in the parish prison. She only ended up doing three months. She would come to church to visit me, and we would flirt and hold hands. And I might steal a kiss from her. We quickly launched a full-blown romance in prison. After seeing her about three times we realized we knew each other from the outside world. When Linda and I moved into our first house in Shreveport, while I finished nursing school, our next-door neighbors were a geologist and his wife, who had taken in their niece. Her parents were troubled, and since shit rolls downhill, she was troubled, too. At age fifteen, she was admitted to the hospital where I worked. As a courtesy, and a neighborly gesture, I popped by her room one day to check on her. I had suddenly realized she was my neighbor's niece! She was fifteen and I was twenty-four the first time we met. At the time, I didn't give her a second thought. But now she was eighteen and in jail for credit card fraud, and I was in jail for selling cocaine. It seemed like a great match to me!

Just as our new love affair was blossoming, Melanie got released. Not long after, I got good time and was able to return to Odyssey House to finish the drug rehabilitation program. Keep in mind, I had left the borders of Odyssey House for six months. Even though I had been in prison they really had no idea what I had been up to. So almost immediately they started peppering me with questions and badgering me about what I did in prison and asking if I was sure about my statements. They decided they couldn't take a chance by letting me back in as a Level Two resident and made me start the whole program over again, but I moved quickly back to Level Two status.

When I was a Level Three, we started working on one of those big fancy projects by affluent donors. They owned an old building on Royal Street in the French Quarter and wanted to open a bakery where Odyssey House residents could work. The building needed a major overhaul. Me and a couple of other guys who had construction experience started the remodel. They paid for all the equipment, and we worked for free until we had created a quaint little bakery. It was a good program for Odyssey House and a pretty good business to boot. They had a French pastry chef who made andouille sausage croissants and croissants of all kinds. The little bakery gained popularity quickly. We even started renting a booth during the New Orleans

Jazz Festival and sold desserts all day. Every day there was a steady stream of people in front of the booth buying food. They would buy anything we had for sale after waiting in line that long. They probably made at least $15,000 that weekend, and in 1980 that was a lot of money. There was a family who rented the booth next to us every year and sold chicken and vegetable plates for about $5. They told me that their whole family worked the jazz fest weekend every year. When Jazz Fest was over, they took big family vacations all over the world because they made so much money.

We also worked on a house in the French Quarter near Commander's Palace in the garden district. Every morning I would take the streetcar to work where I met a crew of guys to work on a massive two-story house. We converted the house into a condominium by basically splitting it down the middle. We created two two-bedroom apartments and added on an addition to the back of the house. We worked hard and the work was good. I eventually made Level Four during this time but making Level Three was the best and most rewarding level to reach. When I made Level Three, that meant Melanie could come and visit me. She would come down to New Orleans just to see me. By this point in the program, I could go outside with her. It was very special to me, and I was starting to fall hard for her.

Before the duplex project was complete, I was released as a Level Four with permission to go back to Shreveport. There was a branch of Odyssey House there for Level Four residents who were scheduled to graduate from the program. It was like an outpatient facility. I got a job at Schumpert Medical Center,

125

and I felt like I was in fucking heaven! I was back working as a respiratory therapist, and Melanie and I were getting more serious in our relationship. I still had probation requirements, including surrendering urine for drug testing on a regular basis, and I had a written assignment due soon. The assignment was essentially a thesis type paper on your life, which you had to be able to defend to the Odyssey House staff.

Things were rocking along pretty smoothly, and it felt like I was well on my way to getting my life back, and in record time. But I screwed up just a little, and it turned out to be a lot more than I bargained for. I smoked a little pot and failed my urine test. They wanted me to completely start the Odyssey House drug rehabilitation program all over, but I said no fucking way. I decided to take my chances in court. I think I knew deep down that I would never finish the Odyssey program. Only a handful of people ever got through the whole thing. It was like they tried to keep you longer and longer, and that was probably because Odyssey House made money off the residents. It was all a big lie. They just wanted you to learn to play the game. The program was about learning to say and do the "right things" at the right time. I just couldn't live like that.

Chapter Ten: The Whole Twenty

One day, Superman was flying around the world, enjoying himself and the views. He flew down to the southern region of the world, near the Brazilian coast. He saw Wonder Woman lying on the beach completely naked. Her legs were spread open, so Superman said to himself, "Hmmm, I think I'll go down there and get me some Wonder Woman. So, he swooped down and like a flash he was gone. As Superman took off again, the Invisible Man lifted himself up off Wonder Woman and said, "Damn, my ass is sore."

Several weeks after I failed my drug test, I had a probation revocation hearing. It seemed highly likely the judge would amend his initial sentencing, especially since it was my first offense, and other than smoking a little pot, things had been going good on my end. I had already served two years of my original sentence by way of Odyssey House and the parish prison. Other than this one infraction, I had not been in any legal trouble. I felt pretty confident about the hearing until I noticed Judge Ballard, the man in charge of my destiny, was nodding off on the bench during the hearing. When he woke, at least long enough to dispense my sentencing, he gave me the whole twenty! To say I was shocked and distraught would be an understatement. I was going to prison for twenty years essentially for smoking a joint, but officially for a first-time felony offense of distributing three ounces of cocaine.

Do not pass go. Do not collect $200. Go straight to jail. I was furious, to put it lightly. I felt a lot like the invisible man on the beach. My ass was sore! That self-righteous son of a bitch couldn't be bothered to keep his eyes open during my hearing, let alone listen to the evidence, but used his rank and authority to destroy me. You've heard of "sleeping judges," who are altogether too conscious of their reelection campaigns, but Judge Ballard was literally nodding off on the day my life was taken from me. I wanted to slap that dirty bastard's face, on both sides, then watch him try to turn the other cheek! Something happened inside of me that day in the courtroom that has stayed with me all these years. I was angry in a way that was completely foreign to me. No matter how much time passes, I still get mad as hell when I think about it. I had developed a sense of hate that has yet to be bested by another human over the course of my lifetime. I will never get over what Judge Ballard did to me that day, and I am sure I was not the only one to suffer at his hand.

They shackled me up and put me back on the van headed for the parish prison. My attorney, Weldon Jack Jr., filed a writ for an "out of time" appeal based on excessive sentencing for a first-time offense. It was granted but it technically took a year and a half to get a hearing at the Supreme Court. Right to a speedy trial, my ass! So, it was back to parish prison life where I remained on the unconvicted side while the writ was filed, and I awaited my appeal. And even though jail time is much different in the parish prison in comparison to doing time in the Louisiana state penitentiary, this time it felt a little more hopeless than it did when I first arrived. Ask anyone who has ever been to prison, and they will tell you that it's the longest, most drawn out, and depressing time of their life is the first year when you're doing big time. You never get used to doing the time, but at the beginning you wallow in the struggle and the depression chisels away at your faith in humanity and even your own humanity. It's sobering in a way that makes you wish you wouldn't wake up every day in your cell. Most people cannot hold on to a rapidly fraying rope like that, and they sure can't pull themselves out of the despair associated with prison. Offenders who cannot set a goal and work towards it every day, just don't make it. And the ones who do slide by and pay their debt to society, many of them reoffend and are cast right back into the system they spent years trying to put behind them. And yet, judges hand time out like its candy. Whether it's five, ten or twenty years, or even a life sentence, there is no hesitation when throwing humans away into their broken system. The broken system happens to be a major moneymaking machine. A convicted felon's bad fortune is another man's wealth. Had I not been a driven hustler who refused to quit, and totally dedicated to my own success, my life may have ended during that first year after the revocation hearing. At the very least, it would have turned out a lot differently.

Normally when you receive a felony conviction you have one year to file an appeal. However, if you can prove that the circumstances did not warrant an appeal at the time, but circumstances have since changed from the time of your conviction, then you have the right to ask for a new appeal even though the time frame has lapsed. Jack Jr. also filed a writ regarding excessive sentencing, and it was approved about eight weeks later, signaling that I had been granted an appeal. Jack Jr. was quite brilliant. Of all the many brilliant people I have met in my life, I am sure as hell glad my attorney was one of them! He was the first attorney in the United States to appeal a death sentence on the basis of posttraumatic stress disorder (PTSD). A Vietnam war vet named Wayne Felde had killed a Shreveport police officer after an alleged improper full body search led to him being arrested and put in the back of the police cruiser. Once locked in, Felde claimed he had a flashback to Vietnam, which he said triggered the sensation of danger, and the experience transported him back mentally to the war zone. Felde managed to get his gun and shot the cop from the back seat of the car. Back then, no one really had a firm grasp on the power of post-traumatic stress, and the U.S. Supreme Court did not reverse the sentence—death by electric chair. Even Felde's sister, Flo, who loaned him the gun got five years hard labor for loaning him the gun that killed the officer. He was executed March 15, 1988.

My appeal went straight to the Louisiana Supreme Court. Jack Jr. gave me the scoop when it was all over. He told me that all seven judges were on the bench that day. Typically, there were five on the bench, but on occasion all seven were in court. He gave his argument on my behalf, and District Attorney Robert Gillespie followed his argument with assertions of a fair sentence. Chief Justice John Dixon asked Gillespie how many years he thought John De Loreon was going to get for buying tons of cocaine from the FBI. Gillespie quickly pointed out that the federal statute had absolutely no bearing on Louisiana law, to which Dixon said, "Yeah, but it doesn't make it any more fairer, does it?" Jack Jr. said he knew when Dixon said that to

Gillespie that things were going well, but he was floored by the unanimous decision of all seven judges, ruling the sentence was, in fact, excessive. Today, you can read about the case in the Southern Reporter. It is also used as an example of excessive sentencing, particularly because of the seven to zero ruling.

The wheels of justice do not turn swiftly. I sat in prison for several months waiting to be resentenced, which was apparently the "reasonable" amount of time it took Judge Ballard. He managed to hold off on the sentencing for almost a year, even though my original sentence had been vacated. In prison there's a saying, "Justice' is really just us." Justice rarely exists.

While waiting for my appeal I was transferred out of the law library and placed in the supply room as a trustee. For the most part I would go in each day and do a few hours' worth of work, then we basically hung out and played pinochle all day. My laundry crew consisted of me and three other guys, Frank, Marvin, and Chip. We were all serving big time for various reasons. We picked up all the laundry in those little mesh bags, washed and dried everything, then passed it back out. We handed out uniforms to new prisoners, and made sure mops, brooms and cleaning supplies were delivered to all four sections of the prison. But most importantly, we watched each other's backs. The job was lame, but it got me out of the dorm and into the yard with other trustees. There wasn't a lot of bullshit going on out there. I also ran the concessions at the prison on Saturdays and Sundays. There were four different visitations. I sold coffee, cokes, donuts, sandwiches, candy, and all kinds of junk food to visitors. We took Polaroid photographs for and of inmates and their guests on visitation days. I enjoyed that.

I met a lot of interesting people in prison, and I heard a lot of interesting stories. Everyone has a story. I met people who had been arrested for selling drugs, cop killers, rapists, and everything in between. I struck up a friendship with a guy who was on death row for killing a police officer. He told me about his case and gave me his version of the events one time. It was much more layered and complex than you might think considering he was serving time as a branded "cop killer." He was a member of the Bandidos, living and partying in Shreveport. The Bandidos were some bad dudes in the sense that they were outlaws, but they didn't really bother anyone. They had a house, and the yard was regularly packed with people and bikes. According to him, this prompted a Shreveport police officer to start following him around. He said the officer was practically stalking him in plain clothes and in a civilian car. Everywhere the Bandito went, the off-duty officer seemed to follow him. The last time the officer followed the Bandito it was to the Dragon Lounge in Shreveport. The officer pulled up next to him at a stop light and reached under his seat, and the Bandito pulled out his gun and shot him. At least, that was his story. He got the chair.

This time around there was no coed mingling at the prison. They had shut that down because someone got pregnant. We were not allowed to have any contact with female prisoners. We could see them as they walked by, and we'd scream and holler at them, and they'd scream and holler back at us. You know— prison shit. The money from the concession stand visitations was used to buy a satellite and a VCR for the inmates to watch cable television. We played pinochle all day, took naps, watched porn, but none of that shit helped pass the time. Frank was a carpenter, and I had quite a bit of experience working with my hands, especially in Germany and at Odyssey House. He taught me how to make cabinets, which proved to be an excellent trade for me later down the road. Time crawled at a snail's pace, except for when Melanie came to visit me. Every time she came to see me, time flew by at a pace I had never known possible. As soon as she arrived it always seemed like our time was up before it got started. I cherished the days and the moments that Melanie came to see me. Seeing her was quickly integrated with my desire for success and gave me just one more reason to keep pushing forward.

In 1986, I finally got my day in Supreme Court. My case was originally filed in 1984. I had been sitting in prison for almost eight months unsentenced. The findings of the State Supreme Court regarding my excessive sentencing appeal can be viewed online by searching: 444 So. 2d 1188 (LA. 1984), 82KA2171 State v. Gordon.

Judge Ballard ordered a presentence investigation to see what I had been up to. I wanted to scream, "I've been in prison, you fucking idiot!" While I was waiting to be sentenced, I asked my attorney to file a writ to get that asshole, Ballard, off the case. He was afraid that if the request was denied the judge would give me the maximum sentence out of spite, so we pressed on.

While I was still in prison waiting to be sentenced, my wife, Melanie, went to Superior Grille in Shreveport with my attorney on "two for one margarita night." Back then, they made their margaritas with Everclear. Most people were sauced after one drink. Ask anyone from Texas or Louisiana about those margaritas and they will tell you they were strong. Melanie and Jack Jr. met for dinner to discuss my case and she ended up having too much to drink. Aggravated and a little intoxicated, she blurted out that if Judge Ballard didn't let her husband out, she was going to shoot him with her pearl handle pistol. Melanie was distraught over the situation, but she would never shoot anyone. She didn't even own a gun! That didn't matter to the nearby table of eavesdropping lawyers, one of which happened to be the current sitting Assistant DA. Jack Jr. tried to diffuse the situation, but they went straight to the District Attorney to relay the drunken rant of a woman whose husband was in prison on an excessive sentence. Ballard was smart enough to leave it alone, but they picked up the charge the next morning and Melanie was arrested for public intimidation. The next morning the police showed up at the house and arrested her. They searched the apartment for a pearl handle pistol, but Melanie didn't even own a gun. In the end, she pled guilty to a felony of public intimidation against someone who was not even present at the time of her drunken statement. She got three years hard labor suspended with one year of probation with the stipulation that she attended Alcoholics Anonymous and report to a probation officer. Am I to believe the sitting Assistant DA was intimidated by a drunk woman a few tables over? Am I to believe the DA who was not present was intimidated? Not a chance. This would never have happened if the DA had not used his power to bend the rules to his advantage. For instance, if you and your neighbor have an argument and your neighbor said, "I'd just like to shoot you!" in a moment of rage, you could not call the police and have him arrested. An average citizen would have to wait for shots to be fired before the law intervened. Abuse of power must not go unchecked.

When the judge arrived, he was visibly angry. He entered the courtroom complaining and made the comment that the Louisiana Supreme Court was forcing him to reevaluate and re sentence. It was beyond Ballard's capacity to admit that he had made a mistake and his devotion to ruining my life still seemed to burn hot. Therefore, in the spirit of resistance and a show of power, he then gave me the maximum number of years he could without it being overturned, which was 12 years. He read from his notes verbatim regarding the maximum allowed time per offense. I got twelve years! He even tried to take away the two years I had already done through Odyssey House and time served before my hearing, but he failed. That was never an option, but it didn't stop him from trying. The state cannot take good time away, and therefore I was eligible for parole right away. The entire room seemed to shift, and the sentencing began to feel deeply personal between Judge Ballard and me. It was hard to believe that he was so dedicated to ruining my life to the fullest extent of which the law would allow. For years I wondered where his passion for punishing me came from because he seemed to delight in it. Despite my service to the country, my education and career achievements, or the fact that I had children, my life meant nothing to that man. I was a lost cause and had no value in his eyes. Giving me the harshest sentence possible could have sealed my fate had I not been a man of grit and determination.

Experience creates expertise, but even without it, people are opinionated about the United States prison system. Having spent time in the system, I have firsthand experience and I sure as hell have opinions about the functionality and corruption of the fragmented system. While I am not asserting that I should not have been held accountable for my actions, I will assert, and even advocate for reform. That said, every case is unique, and there are some genuinely evil people in this world who have no desire to change their lives for the better. But at the end of the day, should one man be the judge of another man or woman's fate? After all, an elected official is human, and no one among us is infallible. Even the man sitting on the bench is a mere mortal, and because of this he is susceptible to having human emotions, and therefore susceptible to ruling under the influence of his own humanness. And even though that's just the "nature of the beast," as they say, it's worth noting that beast is human.

Right now, the American Justice System holds almost 2.3 million people in state prisons, federal prisons, juvenile correctional facilities, local jails, immigrant detention facilities, state psychiatric hospitals, military prisons, and civil commitment centers. There is an enormous and continuous churn in and out of correctional facilities. Every year, approximately 600,000 people enter the prison system, but people go to jail 10.6 million times each year. People in jail have not been convicted. Some will make bail in a matter of hours, while some will remain behind bars until their trial because they were too impoverished to make bail. Perhaps more important than the incredible volume of churn is the question of how much of mass incarceration is a result of the war on drugs? Drug offenses account for approximately half a million incarcerations and nonviolent drug offenses define the federal prisons system. There are over a million drug arrests annually, many of which lead to prison sentences—all of which will be set up to fail upon reentry into this so-called civilized world, most likely for a low-level offense, such as technical violations of probation and parole. Since 1971, when President Nixon declared a war on drugs, to the 1980s when President Reagan expanded the reach of the war on drugs, until about 2014, incarcerations have soared over 1,000%. Over the last five decades, countless lives have been ruined over nonviolent drug offenses in America. Worse yet, of those 2.3 million people incarcerated in American correctional facilities, over 200,000 prisoners are suspected to have been wrongfully convicted. Over the last 25 to 30 years, there have been over 2,000 exonerations, including 200 from death row. They've only scratched the surface. The number of people in prisons in America is a direct reflection of our society and a growing conservative movement that claims its side upholds the gold standard of freedom and morality.

When I was a kid growing up in south Louisiana, it didn't seem like the law and the people who enforced it intended to ruin a person's life. These days officers seem to be interested in arresting as many people as possible, district attorneys are preoccupied with conviction records, and judges are far too eager to lock people up without analyzing the total sum of a person's life. The system doesn't care about your quality of life while serving a sentence, and it damn sure doesn't consider the quality of life on the other side of a prison sentence.

A single person should not hold the destiny of another's life in their hands alone. It's too easy to wrongfully convict a person, which is why I believe a panel of judges should assimilate to determine the fate of another human's life. When you're wrong, you're wrong—regardless of the position you hold. Adding additional insight from other people would help the accused have a better chance for an unbiased and impartial sentencing. I also favor an appointment system for district attorneys, without consideration of their political leanings. This entire country has been divided by politics, and whether a district attorney is a democrat or republican should not factor in as much as it does in prosecution.

It's all a bullshit game. The person on the end of a conviction will have to answer for their mistake for the duration of their life, even long after they have paid their debt to society and served their time. Convicted felons, many with absolutely no skills, cannot find gainful employment after being released from prison. Unable to work and discriminated against, how are convicted felons expected to get a toehold in society, let alone thrive and meet their potential? The answer is— they're not. The system depends on felons to reoffend, so they can welcome them back with open arms while pockets are padded.

The thing about convicted felons, particularly nonviolent drug offenders, is they aren't so different from everyone else. Probably every other person you know uses drugs of some sort.

Whether they obtain theirs legally via prescription or in a shady motel parking lot doesn't make much difference at the end of the day unless you get caught. The kind of high you're chasing, and whether or not you get caught, are basically the only two differences from one user to the next. Yet, those who don't get caught, or who use their connections to get out of legal trouble, are all still just addicts like the unlucky bastards who do get caught.

As one such unlucky bastard, I spent several years rotting away in a parish prison. The food was awful, and it was so boring. When I first arrived, we had oatmeal every day for breakfast, but after the first meal of the day it was beans and rice for lunch and dinner. Not long after I got to prison, I had my first holiday meal. Thanksgiving was a big deal to all of the prisoners, but I had a hard time being thankful for my turkey neck dinner. Someone had donated a bunch of turkey necks, you know, the piece most folks typically discard. They cooked up those turkey necks, served them on a bed of rice with some giblet gravy. I ate that turkey neck that I wasn't particularly grateful for, and I'll never forget it. I spent more time spitting out bones than chewing meat. And while I did not give thanks for that turkey neck, I was definitely thankful that times changed swiftly upon my arrival. The food seemed to improve almost overnight. We started having breakfast options, complete with menus. Chicken and beef started appearing on plates. Things were changing! It looked like they were finally going to have to treat offenders like human beings because a lot of attention was being directed at the country's correctional facilities. People on the outside were beginning to make a lot of noise about it. They were going to have to take care of us, otherwise, we would have all been better off dead.

I fully recognize that my time in prison could have been worse. I didn't have it so bad, but I longed to be back at the hospital and to hold Melanie in the free world. We truly connected in a way that I had never experienced, so I asked her to marry me. A woman who would marry a man serving twenty years had some serious balls. We both knew it was risky, but we both knew it was right. Melanie was twenty-one and I was about thirty. She was sexy as hell, and we got along famously! A day did not pass that I could not wait to start our life together on the outside. Hell, a day did not pass that I could not wait to be on the outside with or without her, but I certainly preferred the latter.

Being a trustee garnered me a little favor with some guards and granted me a few liberties that other inmates didn't have. I could pretty much move about the prison freely, with the exception of maximum security, unless I had specific orders to be there. My trustee clout really paid off on my wedding day. Melanie and I got married by a pastor in the front office at the prison during visitation hours. They took our photo with the Polaroid, and I still have it today. One of the sergeants who was working visitation liked me. He helped us steal about twenty minutes to consummate our marriage by locking us in a room together. This was of course highly irregular, but they did it for me. The guards were good to me, but I especially appreciated their kindness that day.

That said, I would be remiss if I did not tell you there were some real jerks working as guards over the years, too. The one I hated the most was a guy named Charlie. He was a thin fellow with a mustache, and I think he came to work every day to feel powerful and treat prisoners like shit. It was probably the only place in the world where he felt like he was better than someone and he seemed to get great joy out of making our lives miserable. You could be minding your own business, writing on a piece of paper, and he would walk up and take it from you and throw it away. He was a real dick, but fortunately most guards weren't like that idiot. In fact, most of them were very nice people. After I got out of prison, one of my neighbors ended up being one of the guards, who had worked there while I was serving my time. I knew him as Popeye while I was in prison. He was always a fair and considerate man. He later became a sheriff's deputy when he got closer to retirement.

Six years and eight months after that fateful day at the Riverside Inn that landed me in the parish prison, I made parole again. They shipped me over to Monroe for the hearing, and my life started over. This time I was determined not to fuck it up.

Chapter Eleven: I Beg My Pardon

When I finally made parole, my attorney said to me, "If you ever get out of this situation, you should go to California where they'll understand you." I did exactly the opposite and eventually ended up as far away from California as possible—in Texas. Some days I wish I had listened to him. But starting over across the country was just not in the cards for me. I am grateful for the work Jack Jr. did for me and others like me, and far worse.

The day I reentered the free world, they shackled me up and transported me to the courthouse in downtown Shreveport, where I was set up with a parole officer and released. I was a free man again! The first thing I did was buy a coke. I hadn't bought a coke from a coke machine in a long time. I put my money in the machine and gave the Coca-Cola Classic button a good push. The cold red can shot out of the machine, and I gulped freedom.

Freedom aside, I was still so damn angry, and I stayed that way for a long time. I had been angry for years in prison, but it did not dissipate upon parole. I knew the road ahead was long and hard, and I was pissed about it. I was still furious with Judge Ballard for giving me an unreasonable sentence. I thought about that smug prick way more often than I would like to admit. I often wondered about his demons and how tormented he must have been to come for me the way he did. It always felt so incredibly personal. One day when that self-righteous prick crossed my mind, I had a revelation. It occurred to me that he must have someone in his life who struggled with addiction. I knew nothing about Ballard beyond my experience with him in the courtroom. The revelation seemed to help me rationalize why he had given me an obscene sentence and treated me like scum of the earth. I found satisfaction and consolation in believing there was an actual reason that dirty sonofabitch had ruined my life.

It was time to take back my life. One of the very first things I had to do was get a job. Going straight back into nursing was not even close to being an option, but I had some other skills and found work as a handy man. My longtime friend from Schumpert Medical Center, Sarah Boyd's husband Joe, hired me as a painter. I was grateful for the work, and he kept me on for a few weeks making $10 an hour. I got another job as fast as I could, to get Joe off the hook because he really didn't need me; he was just doing me a favor. Later on in life I was eventually able to repay him for his kindness. The next job I had was for the daughter of a very affluent Shreveport family who lived on King's Highway. She hired me to remodel her kitchen cabinets, and I did some other handiwork for her. She liked my work and passed me on to her sisters. Between all of them I stayed busy and working for the next year. I had a modest, leaking workshop down the street from our house. It was cold and wet, but at least I had a place to put my saw, wood pile, and tools. It was easy to get to, a shelter to work under, and all I could afford. Melanie's father worked for Sears as a repo man. He found me an old

Econoline Van that was due to be auctioned off. I went down to the credit union and borrowed $600 and turned it into a work van. I worked out of the back of that thing for a few years.

I also reestablished a connection with my children and made arrangements to pay child support and see them every other weekend. One weekend, I took the kids down to see my mother in south Louisiana in my old Mercury Monarch the State had attempted to seize. It had a lot of miles on it and burned oil pretty bad, but I bought some extra oil, and we took off. On the way, Tracy and Brian were bickering and arguing in the back seat like typical kids. I was acting like a typical father, saying things like, "Don't make me pull this car over." Well, at one point I did have to pull over to put some more oil in the car. Having been in prison, I was behind the times. This was the first oil I had ever purchased in a plastic container. On the container it said, "Easy Pour." Well, it wasn't. Oil got all over the motor and me. I was frustrated and swearing loudly, "Goddamn Easy Pour, my ass!" When I got back in the car the kids were solemnly sitting in silence. A few seconds went by, and they just started busting out laughing at me. "Easy Pour, my ass," became something my children and I still laugh about and still say.

In the meantime, in between all the handyman jobs, I still dreamed of going back to nursing. I had written a letter to the state nursing board, requesting to go back to work on a trial basis while I was on parole. The woman and longtime board member who intercepted my letter was named Sister Lucy Leonard. She sent a denial letter stating they would not consider returning my license until I completed my debt to society. That wasn't what I wanted to hear, but at least I knew something and had a better idea of when I might be able to return to nursing. Nursing aside, respiratory therapy was still going strong and did not require a license, but that was set to change within the next few years.

I needed to get my foot back in the door before the medical field changed too much. All I knew to do was to return to my roots where people had known me before my addiction took over my life. I went back to Schumpert Medical Center to where John Hydell had hired me on the night shift before I went to prison. John was my friend, knew my work ethic, and it did not hurt my cause that he had moved up the ranks and was senior vice president of the hospital at that time. I went to him and asked him if he could hire me back on at the hospital in some way. He told me he would talk to some people at the hospital, but they came back with a resounding no. I told him I understood, but I was like a dog with a bone. I just kept showing back up, asking for a job. John would say no, and I'd tell him I'd be back soon. I was relentless. One day when I went to see John, the new respiratory therapy director, George, was in his office and we struck up a conversation. I explained that I was trying to get my life back together and there was nothing I wanted more than to come back to the hospital and get my license back. I went back to John's office begging for a job three or four more times, and finally, George talked to him. He asked John if the hospital could just hire me on as relief, and that's what they did. There was such an incredible shortage at the time, that even though I had been hired on as relief I was able to work full time.

Perseverance pays off. Not only had I gotten my foot back in the door, but almost immediately I was able to step fully into the room through full time work. I decided to bite the bullet and went to the credit union again. This time I borrowed enough money to pay for tuition to Northwestern State Medical School's eight week accelerated respiratory therapy registry program in Chicago, Illinois. I knew the clock was ticking and that an unlicensed registered respiratory therapist would soon be a thing of the past and replaced b testing and licensing protocol changes. Northwestern guaranteed students who enrolled in the intense course would pass the certification. Respiratory therapy school was taught by the experts, including various authors of the *Essentials of Respiratory Therapy*, including Craig Max, Steve Dumas, and Barry Shapiro. Shapiro was a creative anesthesiologist who pioneered the use of positive end expiratory pressure (PEEP/CPAP). These guys were brilliant! We were legitimately learning from the best of the best. These guys wrote the 'respiratory therapy bible,' which is essentially why they guaranteed anyone who took the course would pass the certification. We had eight hours of lecture five days a week, with tests every Tuesday and Thursday. Every class was a real ball buster. We covered a ton of material every time we met. I roomed with a guy from Boston while I was in Chicago, and we hung out the whole time. All we did was study and go out to eat for eight weeks.

As soon as I got back to Shreveport I signed up for the certification and registry test and I passed it with flying colors. I came in right under the wire of licensure. The State Board felt compelled to issue me a probationary license because I was working and continuing my education. I'll never forget how happy I was when my license came in, even though it had "Probation" stamped across it. I knew it could be revoked at any moment should I screw up, but I was completely dedicated to my goal. I worked hard and within three years I made team leader at the hospital. Shortly after that, I became the ICU coordinator because I had the most experience out of everyone.

Things were going good— really good. And they went even better once my parole ended. I had paid my debt to society in full after 12.5 years. At that time, I was able to get my probationary respiratory therapy certification changed to a regular status just like everyone else. I had come a long way! I had my life by the balls as I rebuilt what was mine. There was still a long way to go because I intended to go back to nursing, come hell or high water.

Once I finally started making some decent money, Melanie and I bought a house in South Highlands in Shreveport. South Highlands was a huge neighborhood. It was built as an expansion of South Shreveport in the 1930's. It was a premier community full of nice mix-matched houses. You might see two-story brick homes scattered among shotgun houses and bungalows. Built in 1935, the house I found had a lot of character. I saw a lot of potential in the house, but it needed some serious love. Luckily, I had the skills to flip the house. I paid $68,000 for it and slowly but surely remodeled it. I tore out walls, hallways, and rewired the entire house. I removed years and layers of paint from the outside with a disc sander. It took over two years, but eventually I had it looking so nice and smooth with a new paint job that my neighbors thought I had put vinyl siding on the house. The house was a great home for us, and I was proud of the work I had done.

All the while, I had been preparing to get off parole. I had filled out pardon hearing paperwork and had it ready to go into the mail. I needed a pardon. I felt like it was the only thing that could truly help me right the universe and climb back to the top and stay there. As soon as my parole ended, I petitioned both the Louisiana and Texas nursing boards and set up an appointment to appear before the boards. Quite a bit of time had passed. I didn't need an attorney to petition the nursing boards to reinstate my license. My drug screens had all been negative the entirety of my parole, and my work ethic vouched for itself. I submitted all the "evidence" to the boards to verify my success, but they balked.

"Well, Mr. Gordon, you've been out of nursing for quite a while. Why didn't you apply for your license earlier?" asked one board member.

I whipped out my letters to and from Sister Lucy Leonard, and said, "I tried, but Sister Lucy Leonard told me I couldn't until my parole had ended."

They didn't particularly want to reinstate my license, but they were backed into a corner. They ordered me to take thirty continuing education hours and do some reporting, all dependent upon a ton of stipulations. Once I had completed the assignment and satisfied the board, they would reinstate my registered nursing license, which took about a week or two for me to complete. As soon as Louisiana reinstated my registered nursing license I appeared before the Texas nursing board and received my Texas nursing license as well.

I had made an application to the parole board prior to having my licenses reinstated knowing it would take them several months to process it. I wanted to have all my ducks in a row before I walked in there, and I did. I even had support. My family drove into Baton Rouge from Cut Off to stand behind me that day. It meant a lot to me to have Melanie and my family there.

Finally, the parole board called my case. I went to the front of the room and a member of the board asked where my attorney was. I told him I didn't need an attorney because I wasn't asking for anything other than a pardon. I showed them the documents ensuring I had completed 12.5 years and paid my debt to society. I explained that my Louisiana registered nursing license had been reinstated, that I was also licensed in Texas, and I had become a respiratory therapist. I explained to them that I had been in anesthesia school but would never be able to fulfill my dream with a felony on my record, and I wanted to return to the workforce with the ability I had before my addiction took over my life. They seemed to like everything I said, so they made a recommendation for a full pardon!

Now, remember that the wheels of justice turn ever so slowly, and therefore almost a year passed with no word on the pardon. Governor Edwin Edwards, the record setting four term governor who did a stint in federal prison for bribery, was known for his quick wit, womanizing and gambling, and he was no stranger to controversy. Known to be a glib and gambling fellow, the governor offered two to one odds that he wouldn't be convicted and joked that he could outlive any sentence that may come down. (A maximum sentence on all 50 of the counts he was charged with added up to about 250 years.) He once bragged that the only way he could lose an election was if he were caught in bed with either a dead girl or a live boy. He spared Klansman, David Duke, no jabs when he told people the only thing that they had in common was that they had both been wizards beneath the sheets. Governor Edwards was an interesting cat who never lost his Cajun accent. I just kept hoping that sometime between all his escapades that he would get around to signing my pardon before he left office.

One day, my mother called and asked if I had received my pardon. I told her I may never get it because Governor Edwards needed to sign it, and he may never sign it. That's when my mother decided to call in a favor. She had grown up with a guy in Cut Off who had gone on to become a very good businessman. He was currently serving as an aid to Governor Edwards. So, she just called up to the governor's mansion and got her old friend on the phone. She told him I needed a pardon, and he said I would have to go to the pardon board. My mother quickly informed him that I had already been to the pardon board, and that the recommendation letter had been sitting on the governor's desk for almost a year. Seven days later, via registered mail, I received a gold seal pardon from the Governor of the State of Louisiana. I was incredibly happy, and I thought all my problems had been solved with the stroke of the governor's pen. It seemed like everything was behind me. I was ready to ride life's highway paved by the power of a pardon. The law was on my side now!

I was fucking wrong! For all intents and purposes, I basically had nothing more than some fancy paper and lip service. A pardon acknowledges a conviction and removes all punishment for it, even if the time has already been served, and forgiveness is entered into the record. But you can't get that sort of forgiveness in the real world. You can't make people understand they should not discriminate against people who have served time, even if they received a gubernatorial pardon. The truth is, a lot of the same people who judge those who have served time have done the same exact things, but they didn't get caught. People who are convicted of felonies often resolve to being a criminal because it is almost impossible to move on. Very few have the stamina and the willpower to overcome their mistakes. Pardon aside, ex-offenders have to answer for their crime again and again when they reenter society and try to enter the workforce because they are required by law to disclose any past criminal history. In other words, a pardon is symbolic and protects you legally from discrimination. You have to be smart enough to know how to use the pardon. The power of a pardon doesn't seem as mighty once you realize that it doesn't protect you from the cruelty of society. Regardless, I was still incredibly grateful to Governor Edwards for signing my pardon. He took a chance on me and there isn't a day that goes by that I don't feel grateful for his generosity.

Life kept moving on, and it seemed to move faster and faster every single day. After I received my pardon, my youngest son, Evan, was born, and Melanie eventually went to nursing school. I was working as a night shift supervisor where I made schedules and took about half a patient load in the ICU. I was spending a lot of time at home remodeling our house. We were living a very nice and happy existence.

Back at work some of my friends and colleagues had started nurse practitioner school. I knew I didn't want to be on the other end of that taking orders. I wanted to move up and be a leader, so I enrolled in graduate school through Northwestern State University. They had a great program for working nurses. I was able to schedule myself off on Fridays and Saturdays for class. I took six hours a semester for the next three to four years and knocked out my master's degree. After I completed all the core courses, I had to pick a career track. I had three choices: nursing administration, nursing education or nurse practitioner. I chose the nurse practitioner family practice track. I did my clinicals in Shreveport and the rest of my clinicals were done in Coushatta, about thirty minutes from Shreveport. It was a privately owned local hospital off Interstate 49, situated along the Red River and a physician owned hospital. It was owned by an older physician who was getting ready to retire. Within the hospital, he also had a family practice connected to the hospital where five other physicians practiced.

He had quite a bit of money and did damn well as he pleased. I guess when you own a hospital you can bend a lot of rules. One rule that cannot be bent is x-raying horses in a hospital. He was an American Quarter Horse enthusiast and owned several. The day he walked into the hospital leading his horse into the x-ray room all hell broke loose. Someone filed a report and he got in some deep shit over that. You can't just trot into a hospital with your animals, even if you own it.

While I was in Coushatta, I trained with a great doctor named Robert Hernandez, who was the only internal medicine physician at the hospital. Before a patient can be admitted into the hospital, they must have an internal medicine consult. Since Robert was the only one available that meant students got a lot of great experience with new admissions, dictating histories and physicals, and writing in mission orders. We had the opportunity to see patients at the hospital and have follow ups in his clinic.

Before I finished nurse practitioner school the grad program required us to publish a retrospective research study as a team. My team reviewed charts and analyzed criteria on hyperlipidemia and treatment. After graduation, one of my research study team members, Kathleen, and I decided to apply for jobs with a gastrologist group in Shreveport. I worked for them a little while and soon turned in my resignation at the hospital to start the first private hepatitis C clinic in Shreveport. We worked out a deal with the local hospitals and got them to run an ad for a public meeting on hep C. We got a food tray together and headed to the hospital thinking we would be happy if twenty people showed up. About 150 people showed up. We were astonished! So many people needed testing or treatment. At that time, interferon studies were being conducted for the treatment of hep C and drug companies were paying for enrollment. The practice made thousands of dollars per person enrolled in the study. Our job was to meet new potential hep C patients, diagnose them, enroll them in the study, and track them periodically through follow ups. People who were in the program came three times a week for injections, or we wrote them prescriptions that they administered at home. It was a very interesting job, Monday through Friday, and I was home every night. Things seemed to be going well.

Melanie and I were sailing along. Our house was almost finished, and I loved my new job. I had been on the job three months when I received a letter from the Louisiana state board of nursing in 1998. It said no one in the state of Louisiana was eligible to apply for a nursing license if they had a felony conviction. I thought to myself, "What the hell does this have to do with me? I have a pardon." I placed a call to the Louisiana State Board of Nursing, and they informed me that while they could not revoke my registered nursing license, they were not going to issue me my nurse practitioner license.

I beg your pardon. Or perhaps, better yet, I beg my pardon. It was devastating, to put it mildly.

I had to retain a lawyer to accompany me down to Baton Rouge to meet with the state board of nursing's legal team. I had spoken to several lawyers and all of them believed there was no way I could lose. The one lawyer who did not believe I could win was on the opposing team and wearing a blue and white pin stripe suit. Turns out, the jerk in the pin stripe suit was right. The power of my pardon was powerless against the Louisiana State

155

Nursing Board as they dispensed their final decision not to license me as a nurse practitioner. My heart sank and my mind raced. I could not understand why anyone would go out of their way to prohibit me from bettering myself and being a productive member of society. To this day, I have never experienced anything as painfully crushing to my spirit as this particular rejection.

I'll tell you why people go out of their way to make others miserable. It's because they think they are better than you. I got caught. And when you get caught you bear the burden for everyone. People think they are better than you for all sorts of reasons but almost everyone thinks they are better than you if you've ever been to prison.

I was suddenly unemployed and scrambling to find a solution. I got on the phone to the Texas State Board and asked to speak with someone about licensing nurse practitioners. They asked if I had a gubernatorial pardon, which I did, so they sent me an application. Texas was willing to honor my pardon like everyone should. I wasn't born in Texas, but I damn sure got there as fast as I could so I could get on with my life.

Chapter Twelve: Pardon My Pardon

Everything was changing quickly in ways I had not foreseen. It's easy to obsess over what you wish you had done differently, or what might have been, when you are facing the unknown. Would I have spent so much time and energy on our dream house if it wasn't really going to be our dream house? Would I have gone back to school had I known the state of Louisiana would not grant my nurse practitioner license? Hard to say, but I am glad I did all those things. Today, when I look back at that time and those obstacles, I realize it wasn't the obstacles that mattered the most. What ultimately mattered was how I responded to and navigated those obstacles. I pushed past the fear and disappointment and kept moving towards my dreams. Every day I got up and did the things necessary to move my life forward, even when it was heartbreaking.

I immediately started looking for a job. The gastro group in Shreveport graciously kept me on for a couple of months until the final decision came down to let me go. They couldn't continue to pay me as a nurse practitioner when I was not licensed and couldn't legally perform half of the duties of the role. My mind reeled with regret. I couldn't stop thinking about all the time and money I spent on an education to better myself. This was supposed to be redemption time, but I was lamenting my decision to leave my previous job, which I had been with for almost twelve years. All felt lost in Louisiana. I thought about recreating myself. I even went all the way to New Jersey for a job interview with a company called Schering-Plough in hopes of snagging a job as a hep C drug representative. I bought a topcoat and a leather bag brief case to look the part. I met a woman who was also from Tyler on the way to New Jersey, and who also happened to be applying for the drug rep position with Schering-Plough. Neither of us got the job. We found out that the job had already been closed and the company really had no intention of hiring, but they were always on the lookout for the next drug rep superstar. She and I struck up a friendship and I still occasionally run into her today.

I was growing frustrated. I started reaching out to people who might be able to help me land a job. A pulmonologist I knew from Shreveport told me he knew Dr. David Johnson over in Tyler, Texas was looking for help. He suggested I look there. So, I drove to Tyler, the largest city in East Texas, which isn't saying much. I interviewed with Dr. Johnson at his office. We met and had lunch, then he showed me around and offered me the job. I took it.

Before I left Louisiana, I retained a lawyer and sued the Louisiana State Board of Nursing for refusing to license me. (James Morris Gordon v. LA State Board of Nursing 804 So. 2d 34 (LA Ct. App. 2001). It took approximately two years, but they had to give me my license. The court ruled that they could not withhold it due to my felony because I had a gubernatorial pardon. I kept it active in Louisiana, but never used it again. The law required them to treat me as if I had never committed a crime.

Ex Parte Garland, 71 U.S. 333, 18 L. Ed. 366, 4 Wall. 333 (1866), from which the case the Louisiana Supreme Court, in State v. Lee, quoted the following language as defining the operation and effect of a full executive pardon:

A pardon reaches both the punishment prescribed for the offence and the guilt of the offender; and when the pardon is full, it releases the punishment and blots out of existence the guilt, so that in the eye of the law the offender is as innocent as if he had never committed the offence. *** *If granted after conviction, it removes the penalties and disabilities, and restores him to all his civil rights; it makes him, as it were, a new man, and gives him a new credit and capacity. There is only this limitation to its operation: it does not restore offices forfeited, or property interests vested in others in consequence of the conviction and judgement. State v. Lee, 171 La. At 747, 132 So. At 219220. Considering this description of the operation and effect of the executive pardon, and its endorsement by the highest court of this state, Gordon's restoration to the status of innocence blotted out any existence of guilt, as well as the conviction itself. Therefore, insofar as the decision of the LSBN was based on Gordon's felony conviction, or the underlying facts concerning his guilt with respect to the charged offenses, the decision was erroneously rendered and the ruling of the district court reversing that decision was correct.*

I didn't need the license now that I was in Texas, but that wasn't the point. I wasn't going to let them get off with discrimination.

At first, I was incredibly disappointed and extremely hesitant about moving to Texas. I had come from Shreveport, a thriving city of about 250,000 people and eleven hospitals to live and work in a city where there were less than 100,000 people and only two hospitals. It was a complete culture shock. But the hospitals were very large, about 500 beds each, and they drew from a shockingly large area. At that time, Tyler's population was about 87,000, but at any given time there were probably 250,000 people in the city shopping, working, and visiting people in the hospital. The two hospitals served East Texans who lived within about a two-hour radius. Usually, towns that size do not have a big medical system, but Tyler was an anomaly and it worked out great for me.

I rented an older apartment house right across the street from my office on Broadway. Melanie and I set up the apartment with minimal furniture. I worked all week, then drove home to Shreveport on the weekends to be with my family. I kept thinking I should have at least investigated moving to Austin. East Texas was its own special kind of hell. You might say it is the buckle of the bible belt. But there we were.

We put our dream house on the market on a Sunday. We stuck a 'for sale by owner' sign up in the yard and by Monday we had a contract. We had purchased the house for $68,000 and put about $30,000 into it. My hard work and sweat equity paid off, and we had no problem selling our dream home for more than $150,000.

One afternoon when we were house hunting in Tyler, Melanie and I stumbled upon a house that had been on the market for over a year just as the owner was pulling the 'for sale' sign out of the yard. The house was listed at $260,000. It was a great two-story house, over 3,000 square feet with vaulted ceilings. The guy who owned it was a large man and no longer able to get up and down the stairs. His parents had done well in the oil and gas industry and left him a lot of money, part of which he used to build himself a single-story home. As he was taking the 'for sale' sign down, we pulled in and eventually struck a deal for $196,000, and just like that, we were fulltime Texans.

Almost immediately after I took the job with Dr. Johnson the office manager was fired. He asked if I could run the office, and of course, I said yes, but I needed hospital privileges to both East Texas Medical Center (ETMC) and Trinity Mother Francis. Most Tyler doctors worked at both hospitals. In order to obtain hospital privileges, I would have to go in front of the hospital board to present and apply. Basically, what that equated to was regurgitating all my past life transgressions and how I made amends for my wrongdoings. Nursing licensure applications typically ask if you have ever been convicted of a felony "unless you have a pardon." In fact, it even says if you have a gubernatorial pardon that you may answer "no" to the question. However, that was a crock of shit based on moral turpitude. If you didn't fill out the criminal history part of an application and your employer later found out, you could be fired for lying.

When you apply for hospital privileges you must reveal everything. I had a gubernatorial pardon and a good track record in Louisiana. I went before ETMC's board, and they granted me privileges under the stipulation that I was subject to a drug test at any time. Mother Francis hospital, on the other hand, was a different beast altogether.

An older woman named Cheryl Boss was the medical staff director at the time. I met her when I went in to meet the medical staff and discuss accessing privileges. I only call my friends by their first names, so I will refer to her as Ms. Boss. She was a tiny little lady, but she packed a big ass punch. She looked me dead in my eyes and said, "Mr. Gordon, we don't like people like you with drug convictions working at our hospital." I said, "Ma'am, I have a pardon," but she didn't care. She told me it didn't look good and that I should go work for a while in the community and come back and apply once I had established a local track record. I was pissed but did exactly as she suggested. I returned to the office and told Dr. Johnson I was unable to get privileges at Mother Francis and explained that their medical staff director recommended I come back after I established myself in the community. I kept working at our office and did new patient consults once a week on Wednesday nights in the sleep clinic of our practice. I can't complain about the work. My job was great. I kept working, seeing follow up patients, and rounding at ETMC. I helped run the sleep clinic in our office, which was great extra money.

After about a year had passed, Dr. Johnson asked when I would be able to get privileges at Mother Francis. I called up

Ms. Boss and reminded her of who I was. I told her that I had been working in the community since I last saw her, as she had recommended, and I had returned to apply for privileges. Ms. Boss said, "Mr. Gordon, I've decided not to present you to the board for hospital privileges. If the board refused you, you would never be able to apply here again." I tried to explain that I would understand if I had been denied for a legitimate reason, but she cut me off with a cold reply.

"I just don't want your kind working here," she snarled.

That was it. I wasn't about to let this lady stand in my way or pull some morally superior bullshit. Ms. Boss was not the boss of me! I sat down at my desk and composed a letter to the risk management division of Mother Francis and politely gave them the facts about my conversation and experience with the medical staff director. I asked them to find a way to grant me a hearing no matter what the outcome may be or that I would sue them for discrimination. Seven days later, Ms. Boss gave me a call and said she had decided to grant me a hearing. I told her, "You didn't decide shit, ma'am. I went over your head and told them I was going to sue them for your wrongful actions and discrimination." It was a real moment of fucking glory for me with that self-righteous bitch! Finally, I had privileges at both hospitals, with the same stipulations—a drug test at any time. Work was going great, and I loved my job. I didn't think it could get any better. I was working with Dr. Jonathan Adam Markowitz from California who had trained at the Wadsworth V.A. in Los Angeles. He became my greatest mentor. He taught me more about medicine than I could have learned in two nurse practitioner lifetimes. I will always be indebted to him for the knowledge he shared with me and the encouragement he gave me over the years.

I was really starting to hit a great stride in my professional life when we moved to Tyler. My career was taking off like a rocket, but my marriage was breaking apart like the Space Shuttle Columbia. Melanie was struggling to hold her life together despite my newfound success. Eventually her world just totally fell apart, and therefore so did our marriage around 2006. She had her own issues, as we all do, but they were far outside of my control. We decided to end the marriage after twenty-four years. The first few years Melanie and I continued living together. I wanted to ensure that she and Evan were cared for, but after several years it got so unpleasant that I moved out. Melanie is sharp as a tack; she should have been a lawyer. But the last thing I wanted to do was come home after working a fourteen-hour day and stay up all night arguing with her. Fortunately, getting a divorce was the best possible thing that could have happened to our relationship. She got her life together and I stopped enabling her. Melanie and I remain best friends to this day despite the differences we had at the end of our marriage.

I spent thirteen incredible years at Pulmonary Associates. When we decided to close the office, it took six months. We had over 5,000 files and records that needed to be scanned and documented. My youngest son, Evan, and his friends were tech savvy and took on the task. We closed down the office and Dr. Johnson, Dr. Markowitz, and I went to work for East Texas Medical Center as hospitalists. Dr. Markowitz negotiated my salary by taking two doctor loads and carving out one doctor's salary for me.

We were known to cut up and carry on around the nurse's station. I couldn't resist giving the new nurses a hard time and joking around. I would say things like, "I just read an article that said 40% of American women were on psychotropic medications. It's astonishing that so many women could have mental health problems but worse yet, there are about 60% of women untreated." The nurses would scatter when we came around!

As much as I liked to joke around, I also considered myself a patient advocate. I was always concerned about patient safety and workflow issues. I expected people to do their jobs and I was outspoken about it. And I never stopped caring about the individual or their families who needed medical help. I was never so callous that I didn't care.

For instance, a guy I knew who used to be a physical education teacher was paralyzed in an accident. His entire life was turned upside down in an instant and his grief was intense. I cared for him after his accident, and it was traumatic every time he asked me to kill him. He felt like his whole life was over. Many, many patients have begged me throughout my career to end their lives. It's heavy.

It's strange how an incident can stick with you forever. Once, a little boy about three or four years old came in with an obstruction in his airway. He had inhaled an orange seed that had become lodged in one main stems. We didn't have the high-tech equipment and tools to retrieve objects back then and were unable to remove the seed. The little boy ended up on a ventilator and ended up dying of pneumonia. I was physically unable to go into the boy's room because he was the same age as my son. I thought constantly about his parent's grief. Many years have passed, but I still recall that case very vividly.

Another time, Melanie and I were on I-20, headed to Dallas with her parents, when we saw a horrific accident. One of the children in the accident was probably about nine years old. He had a head injury, and I knew it was fatal because he had no pulse and was not breathing. I knew it was futile, but I kept doing CPR and chest compressions for twenty minutes until EMS arrived. When EMS arrived, they were unable to intubate the boy, so I told them to let me try. The paramedic asked why I thought I could do it and I told him I was a respiratory therapist, and I did them all day for a living. I was able to get the boy intubated and watched him fly away in the helicopter. I never knew what happened to the little boy, but I still think about him. I cried like a baby when that helicopter took off. It was one of the most stressful situations I had ever been in, and I was overcome for the families. It was the most helpless feeling in the world to have a child dying in my arms right in front of my eyes. Giving good care to those in need has always been and will always be my passion. So, to know what to do and how to do it, but not have the tools to execute was crushing. My eyes still fill with tears every time I think about him.

Chapter Thirteen: Chasing My Tail to Find Me

The next five years following my divorce brought a resurgence of partying back into my life. If there was a bar open, I was in it, and if there was a woman involved, all the better. My relationships with women over the next few years ranged from casual sex to committed sex, and even love. Overweight, over worked, and depressed, I considered leaving Tyler after Melanie and I divorced. I contemplated what it would be like to head west towards Austin, and what it would take to establish myself in their medical community. I thought about having to tell my story again and again. With or without a pardon, I would still have to answer for the mistakes of the past. It just wasn't worth it, and oddly enough, life in East Texas wasn't so bad. I had paid my dues in Tyler and climbed the proverbial ladder of discrimination after proving myself again and again.

In 2007, my friend Victoria, who worked for an oxygen supply company, invited me to a Christmas party. Over 100 guests had been invited. I hadn't been there long when I saw a woman walking across the back yard. I could not take my eyes off her. I knew I had to meet her, so I struck out across the crowd to make contact with her, but she disappeared. Closer to Christmas, a drug rep buddy of mine and I met up for drinks at a bar in Tyler called Dakota's. We showed up to the bar in cut off t-shirts, and they wouldn't let us in because there was a black-tie event going on. We went down to Outback and drank there until about 10 p.m., until I got the idea that we should go back to Dakota's. I told my friend everyone would most likely be drunk by then and we could get in. I was right! We slid right in. Low and behold, there at the bar stood the woman who had captured my attention at the Christmas party. She and her friend had both been drinking. Her friend mistook my buddy for some guy named Robert. She came up to him and asked him to forgive her for dipping out on him a few nights ago. He said he could forgive her… if he was Robert. Meanwhile, there she was, standing with her back to the bar, gently perched up by her elbows. I walked up to her at the bar, and she introduced herself to me and struck up some conversation. I had no intention of letting her get away again. I interrupted her and said, "Norah, you're far too beautiful. I have to kiss you." And then I kissed her! I had never done something like that before. It's one of those bucket list fantasies I think every man has. The best part was, she kissed me back! We moved our make out session to the parking lot, and she gave me her number before she left. But when I came calling, she refused to go out with me because she was engaged. I deleted her name from my phone and forgot about her.

Over a year had passed since I had seen her, until one day I saw her at the hospital when she was visiting her ailing father. For the life of me I could not remember her name! I asked everyone I could think of to help me find her name and number, but no one knew. Time passed and I was frequently on the barstool at Dakota's. One day I was having a drink and going through my phone deleting names and numbers. I ran across my buddy's number and decided to call him up and ask if he could remember her name. He couldn't and told me it just wasn't meant to be. I turned around and she was sitting right behind me at a table with a group of people! I moved quickly to her and told her I had been looking for her for weeks. She asked what I was going to do now that I had found her.

What I didn't do was kiss her. That did not work out so well, the first time. Thus began a long running on again, off again relationship, riddled with problems that were outside of my scope or control. When it was good, it was really good. And when it was bad, it was over. It was only bad for me though because she held all the cards. She chose if, and when, we communicated. Long spells of radio silence would eventually be interrupted when she decided she wanted to talk to me, or perhaps when she needed something. I took the bait—hook, line, and sinker—every single time she called. I was completely enamored with her, and she began to remind me of a very "lovely lady." I just couldn't say no.

I took part in setting up both Nurse Practitioner Associations in Shreveport and Tyler. I was invited to speak at the first convention for the State Nurse Practitioner Association Convention in Louisiana. It was gratifying in a way that gave me more satisfaction than any amount of partying or a one-night stand ever could.

After speaking at the state nurse practitioner conference in Louisiana I went to look around the vendor's showroom floor. I happened upon a booth where a woman was selling jewelry. I picked up her card and noticed her last name was Ballard. It was the same last name of the judge who had given me an illegal and excessive sentence for a first-time offense, and effectively changed my life forever. I politely asked her if she knew Judge John Ballard, to which she replied, "Yes, he is my father-in-law." I told her I didn't want to upset her, but I needed to tell her to relay a message to Judge Ballard. I said, "Tell Judge Ballard that no matter how hard he tried to ruin my life, he could not succeed because I was stronger than him. Tell him James Gordon said that." I asked her if her husband had ever had a drug habit, and she revealed to me that he had. It made perfect sense that Judge Ballard's son was having drug problems around the time I was sentenced, and why he would give me such a lengthy sentence. He was transferring all of his anger about his son's issues on to me, and who knows who else, during that time. It was a great freaking moment for me! I asked her to let him know I was doing just fine.

By the middle of 2010 I was blowing and going pretty hard and dating a significantly younger woman. She was thirty-two and I was sixty. She and I traveled to New Orleans for a party and to spend some time with my mother. Early in the day, I began having indigestion but didn't think much of it. We gambled until about 3 a.m., and when we got back to our room, I started having chest pains. Jennifer called 911, and they loaded me up on a gurney and took me out of the Marriot through the kitchen. I didn't let them keep me for observation. The next day we went to my mother's house, where I had another serious chest pain. I decided to have a green dragon mixture for indigestion called in and started heading back to Texas. We got to the Atchafalaya Bridge in Morgan City when I started having

170

incredible chest pain. We pulled over at a little gas station in Burwick, which was at least sixty miles away from the nearest major hospital in Lafyette. My hot young girlfriend went into the bathroom while I figured out what to do. She was in there a long time. I don't know if she was in there doing meth or if she was just taking pictures of herself in front of the bathroom mirror, but I was having intense chest pain in the passenger seat of my little BMW convertible. No one was in the parking lot and there was no sign of my girlfriend. I was writhing in pain and jumping all around that little car. I motioned for the store clerk to come out, but she was unsure, and I am sure scared. I had to have looked like a maniac by this point. I motioned to the bathroom for her to go get my girlfriend. She finally came out and called 911.

I went by ambulance to Morgan City Hospital. It's a little hospital with about sixty beds. The ER doctor gave me some morphine, ran some labs, put me on a heart monitor and observed me overnight. The next morning the doctor came in and said he had scheduled me for a heart cath. My lab work revealed elevated troponin levels and he said we needed to see if there was blockage. I asked if they did interventions at their hospital, but he explained that they only perform heart caths and in the event that there was any blockage, I would be transferred to a larger hospital.

I was absolutely not having that procedure at Morgan City Hospital. I knew better. I made them move me to a hospital where they could do everything at once. I ended up at Thibodaux General Hospital where I received two stints. They were unable to get a balloon in for the third stint that I needed. As soon as I got back to Texas my cardiologist placed the third stint, and over time he placed two more. I ended up with five stints within the period of a year, and I have been cruising along pretty good ever since.

After my heart attack, I began examining my life with a different perspective. It was time to slow down. It was time to grow up...again. It was past time to wise up. This life lesson reminded me of the old story of two bulls.

An old bull and a young bull were sitting on top of a hill watching the cows eat grass below. The young bull was snorting and kicking up dust as he pawed the ground. The young bull said to the old bull, "let's run down there and fuck us a cow."

The old bull turned slowly to him and said, "Why don't we just walk down and fuck them all."

I am older and wiser now, like the old bull. Life is all about maturing and gaining wisdom.

I spent a lot of time with a guy named Jody Hargis. He was my brother from another mother. He was a great friend to me and a great drinking buddy. He convinced me to do something for myself and go scuba diving. He also convinced me to stop drinking so much, although not in the classic intervention style. He moved to Puerto Morelos in Mexico but kept his house in Tyler. It made a great bachelor pad for me while he was out of the country. He married a woman from

Venezuela, and they had a beautiful son. They have been instrumental in my life, and I consider all of them to be part of my family.

My on-again, off-again relationship with Norah, the woman of my dreams, was a tedious back and forth spanning about five years and was often abruptly interrupted over religious beliefs— particularly, my lack of religion. She considers herself a very religious person and it troubled her that I was not religious. In fact, I am an atheist, but it didn't bother me at all that she was, what she referred to as a "believer." When our relationship was interrupted by the "almighty," I tried to fill my time with other women.

Three years later she called me out of the blue while she was on vacation in Costa Rica. At first it really pissed me off because I thought she was there with some guy. I was a real jerk until I realized she was there with her nieces and nephews for a family trip. She told me she missed me and wanted to be with me. And just like that... I was gone again.

Chapter Fourteen: You Never Know

After the Costa Rica connection, Norah and I decided it was time to get serious. We decided beliefs and non-beliefs were non-issues. She was lonely and I was in love. We spent almost the next three years as a committed couple. Norah played a pivotal role in the making of my memoir, and until recently I believed she was my "happy ending." I was wrong. Just like a light switch, she simply turned off our relationship without warning. The day before she delivered the blow, we had talked about spending the rest of our lives together.

At nearly seventy-one years old, the ground shifted under my feet again. I was tired of constantly rebuilding my life in some way. I was tired of learning lessons the hard way. But the lesson that came in my seventh decade taught me something very, very important— You just never know what is going to happen. No matter how much you prepare, you cannot predict what will happen in your life. If you are banking on anyone other than yourself to bring you happiness, you're making a mistake.

There are only three things I know for sure. Miracles are the result of a lot of hard work, tornados come and go as they damn well please, and the American legal system is completely broken. The rest of life is just a series of curve balls being hurled at you, matters of the heart that enrich or impoverish our souls, often both, and the choices we make along a personal evolution. All bets are off otherwise. That said, what I thought was my happy ending, has now become a side note. Time marches on. I'm well acquainted with time, whether it is marching on or standing still. I know all too well the kind of time that passes so slowly you lose interest in keeping track, and I am well-acquainted with the kind of time that passes so quickly you can't keep up. Navigating through the sands of my lifetime has taught me many things and I have seen a lot of change throughout the years. Unfortunately, one area I have not seen enough change in is the American justice system.

I am a reasonable man with reasonable expectations. I tend to trust people and I do my best to treat people fairly even though I have not always been extended fairness. But because I am not wearing a robe and wielding justice, and I am not working to increase a conviction record, my reasonability falls far short of impacting the kind of change that is so desperately needed. Having been in the system I know that it is a 'miracle' in every sense of the word that I was able to find value after paying my debt to society, let alone any level of success. Don't forget, the miracle is the product of hard work, and they do not come easy. I made that miracle happen through determination. That said, even though I managed to reach miracle status, I still must answer for my mistakes to this day. The many miracles I achieved did not exempt me from having to be accountable for a mistake I made while I was in my twenties. I am a reasonable man, and I understand that the general public can't fully comprehend the atrocities of our country's justice system, not having experienced them personally. You can't know, what you don't know.

I've heard people say, "Well, it only affects you if you break the law." That is the rallying cry of smallminded people who cannot see outside of themselves. Almost one in every 100 Americans is imprisoned, and since we know that no man is an island, we know without a doubt that the ramification of a flawed legal system impacts more than those who break the law. The United States holds less than 5% of the world's population, yet we dominate the entire globe with 20% of the word's incarcerated people here in the "Land of the free." With roughly 11 million people behind bars on planet Earth, one out of every five of those prisoners is incarcerated here in the United States. More people are behind bars in this country than the number of people who live in Dallas. If the American prison system was its own city, it would be in the top ten largest U.S. cities. I am a reasonable man, but this is unreasonable.

America has created an entire industry largely based on criminalizing social issues. The industry is a vicious cycle of humanness, inhumanity, and politics driven by greed and power. To make a mistake is human. To judge another person for the rest of his or her life based on one error in judgement is inhumane. According to the Federal Bureau of Prisons, 46% of people who are currently imprisoned in America are in for a drug offense. Changes in law and policy, not changes in crime rates, explain the roughly 500% increase in American prisoners over the last few decades. The results are overcrowding in prisons, fiscal burdens on states, and lifelong oppression for those who serve time. It's best not to get caught up in the wheels of justice, but as we've seen in recent years, even innocent people get caught up because the system is so incredibly flawed. Mere mortals, often guilty of the same or worse than those they are sentencing, dole out punishment for their fellow man and never look back, let alone look towards the future of the offender's life. No one can make me believe that every judge in America hasn't had a bad day and ruled on a matter through the lens of whatever was happening in their life at the time. Maybe a judge has a child struggling with drug addiction and tends to rule harshly because of the impacts his child's addiction has had on his life, or maybe his wife won't sleep with him and he's just in a bad mood. The point is—all of us are fallible. Judges, law enforcement, and District Attorneys are human and make mistakes just like the people they are charged with sentencing, arresting, and prosecuting. The only difference is, they almost never have to answer for it. Too much unbridled power has turned America into the world leader of incarcerations.

For the sake of clarity, and because I am a reasonable man, I want to say that there are people who need to go to prison. Murderers, rapists, and people who hurt other people are at the top of that list, and I believe most people would agree on that. But I also believe that most people would agree that the justice system needs immediate reform.

After all these years I am finally telling my story. I hope to become an advocate for change in America's "IN-justice" system because I want to shine a light on the issues, but I also because I want to inspire people who have been oppressed by the system. I want them to be encouraged to keep pushing forward and to put in the hard work required to make the miracle they need. I also want my children and grandchildren to know about my life, my experiences, who I was, where I came from, and how I became the man I am today. I am still evolving and still rolling with the punches. I am a product of my own making, both good and bad.

For many years I had wanted to find a way to thank Governor Edwards for signing my pardon. One day, in early 2021, I was telling my daughter Tracy that I really wanted to write to him and thank him, but I could not find his address. She told me he was living near Baton Rouge and that she would get his address for me. Tracy came through and located his address. I wrote to Governor Edwards on a Thursday, thanking him for giving me the opportunity to recapture my life and for having put his faith and trust in me. I told him he was a big part of the reason I had been able to succeed. The following Monday, he called me at work to thank me for writing to him. We spoke for several minutes, during which I thanked him again and asked about his young son. It was a great conversation that I will never forget. I am so grateful that I was able to connect with him when I did, because he died just a few months later, right after I retired.

I have apologized to my children numerous times for being a terrible father. More than anything else in my life, I wish I could change that. But we all know you can't change the past, and I believe we have all accepted that and built the necessary bridges to move forward together as a family. As much as we've grown and reconnected, they still do not know everything about my life. For the last few years, I've spent countless hours telling and retelling my life story in order to give my children the opportunity to really know me by telling them the truth about my past.

When my first child, Tracy, was born I fully understood why fathers feel the way they do about their daughters. My son Brian came along shortly after and there was nothing I loved more than holding him in my arms while I rocked him in a swing on the front porch. I loved them both so much it was unbelievable. Despite my love for them, I was neglectful. My addiction took precedence over everything in my life. I will always carry the regret of not being a better father to my children when they were little.

When I got out of prison, the very first thing I did was reestablish contact with my children and set up regular visitation and child support payments. It was difficult because I didn't have steady work, but I was a hustler, and it was very important to me. My two oldest children were greatly impacted by my choices and the repercussions that followed, but of the two, Brian was deeply wounded. There was a brief period while he was in high school that he asked to come live with me, but it was short-lived. He joined the Army, but before he left, I told him I understood why he was mad at me and that I wished I had done things differently. He called once in a blue moon, but we basically became estranged for a while. Tracy was a survivor. She went off to college, and I continued to make direct 'child Support' payments to her to help her get through school at Louisiana Tech. My youngest son, Evan, had a much different upbringing and childhood than my oldest children. For starters,

I wasn't on drugs or in prison, and as you can imagine, that alone made a world of difference.

Years passed and eventually Brian and I had a conversation that changed everything. He told me he was angry that I had not been available for him growing up. He was particularly angry about the lack of time I spent with him after I got out of prison, because I was always at work. He told me that since he had become a father, he understood why I worked so much when he was a kid and that he now respected me for it. The smartest move I ever made as his father was letting him know that I loved him and that I would be there when he was ready to have a relationship; then backing off and not trying to force it. Today Brian and I enjoy a wonderful relationship.

All my children are incredibly intelligent and driven. They have each been successful in their lives and careers, and they are each raising beautiful families. I adore my grandchildren and I love my family. Every time I see them, I am thankful for all the miracles in my life.

At this stage in my life, I am a very vocal person, but for many, many years I was unable to speak out. My career, my freedom, and acceptance all seemed to hinge on keeping my head down and keeping my mouth shut. I was able to have discussions in a professional setting, but I had to mind my Ps and Qs a little more than the average person because of my past. I spent years eating shit politely. Imagine standing in front of someone after you had spent years educating and reforming yourself only to be told, "We don't like your kind here." To

181

believe that people who have served time do not want to come out and be better humans is totally misguided. Years of my life were spent repeatedly proving my value. No one should ever interfere or discourage another person who is trying to better themselves. Today, I challenge people on their views, I challenge administration and coworkers, and I challenge religion. Of course, I do this in a respectful way, but I say things out loud now. I don't let things slide as easily now that I have reached this stage of life. It shouldn't be considered hurtful to tell the truth. And I know it's the truth because often after I've spoken up at work, administration looks at me and smiles in silent agreement. They know everyone knows there is an elephant in the room, and no one wants to come out and talk about the elephant but me. I love saying there's an elephant in the room and asking what we are going to do about it! And while I do feel a greater sense of freedom at this stage in life, I look forward to retirement. I no longer need to work, but I truly enjoy the work and love my career in spite of the general bullshit that happens in the medical field. For instance, customer service has overcome common sense and asserts that everyone should be satisfied just as if they were shopping at Dillard's. Who can or would be satisfied if their loved one died in the hospital? You can return a shirt to Dillard's, but you can't get grandma back if she dies in the hospital. You can't make chicken salad out of chicken shit. For example, if a patient is admitted in the fetal position, the family often expects the patient to leave figure skating. The point is, not everyone will be satisfied, and the reasons will be varied.

I have long since said that the ideal happy ending for my life would be for Louisiana to legalize marijuana and to buy the old parish prison in Keithville that I did my time in and turn it into a marijuana grow farm. If that ever happens, I will give myself an excessive sentence!

You never know what is going to happen in this life, but rest assured, you will have to answer for your reactions. Is it fate? Is it luck? It doesn't matter. The only thing that matters is how you move forward. The universe will ask who you are, and if you don't know, the universe will tell you.

Sometimes our rigidity makes us forget that other people see things in a different light. Things can change so quickly, in an instant, and we can learn from others' experiences. Just ask the four Coonasses who were sitting around one day trying to figure out what the fastest thing in the world is.

"The fastest ting in the world gotta be a thought. As soon as you tink somethin' it becomes a thought right away. There ain't nothin' faster than that," said the first Coonass.

The second Coonass piped up and said, "You know, I tink you're wrong. I tink it's a blink. Because your whole life can change in the blink of an eye.

The third Coonass said, "You all wrong! It's electricity. As soon as I hit the light switch, the light come on. Nothin' is faster than dat."

183

"Y'all all wrong. The fastest thing in the world is diarrhea," said the fourth Coonass. The group laughed, but he insisted. "I'm serious y'all. Last night, dat diarrhea come over me so fast—before I could tink, blink, or turn on the light switch, I shit all over myself."

For instance, just as this book was in the final stages of being published, I was forced into early retirement. You just never know.

Here We Go Again...